Side Lights Upon Bible History

十五

SIDE LIGHTS

BIBLE HISTORY

LONDON
MACMILLAN AND CO.

SIDE LIGHTS

UPON

BIBLE HISTORY

BY

MRS. SYDNEY BUXTON

WITH ILLUSTRATIONS

London

MACMILLAN AND CO.

AND NEW YORK

1892

PREFACE

In writing this little book, it has not been my aim to give any connected account of Israelitish history. I have sought to study the Bible from an outside point of view, and to show where Bible history is interwoven with and affected by that of nations other than the Israelites.

I have throughout used the language of the Bible, and of other ancient records, in order that my readers may be kept as much as possible in "the presence and the power of greatness."

C. M. B.

15 Eaton Place, *May* 1892.

CONTENTS

CHAPTER IV

CHAPTER V

CHAPTER VI

ILLUSTRATIONS

* For the use of these illustrations I am indebted to my kind friend, the late Mr. Murray.

NOTE ON REFERENCES

Berosus and Manetho are quoted from Cory's *Ancient Fragments*, 1832.

Herodotus (H.), in Rawlinson's edition, 1880.

Diodorus (D.), in Booth's translation, 1814.

Rec. refers to *Records of the Past*.

Rec. N. S. ,, ,, New Series. Edited by A. H. Sayce.

"Renan," unless otherwise stated, refers to the *Histoire d'Israel*.

"Stanley," to the *Jewish Church*.

"Josephus," to the *Antiquities of the Jews* (Whiston).

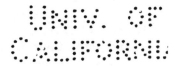

CHAPTER I

" And the Lord planted a garden eastward in Eden; and there he put the man whom he had formed. And out of the ground made the Lord God to grow every tree that is pleasant to the sight, and good for food; the tree of life also in the midst of the garden, and the tree of knowledge of good and evil. And a river went out of Eden to water the garden; and from thence it was parted, and became into four heads."—Gen. ii. 8-10.

THE nations of whom we first read in history lived in the three great alluvial plains[1] of the Nile, of the Tigris and Euphrates, and of the Indus.

It was only in fertile districts, on land which was the gift of some mighty river, that men in a primitive state of civilisation could gather together

---

[1] "Valley plains," says Hegel, "are plains permeated by rivers, and which owe the whole of their fertility to the streams by which they are formed. Such a valley plain is China,— India, traversed by the Indus and the Ganges,—Babylonia, where the Euphrates and the Tigris flow,—Egypt, watered by

B

and form their first communities. Accordingly
we find that in such great river plains men
had gathered into nations, while all the other
peoples of the earth were still wandering about,
living without rule or order, "like the beasts
of the field." [1]

And thus the valley of the Euphrates—Mesopotamia, the "between river country,"[2] the "ager
totius Asiae fertilissimus" of Pliny, the land
where grew *every tree that is pleasant to the sight
and good for food*—became the fruitful mother of
much of the world's earliest thought and culture.

the Nile. In these regions extensive kingdoms arise, and the
foundation of great states begins."—*Phil. of History*, 93.
"On such fruitful tracts as the mouths and middle courses
of rivers, nations could find a permanent home, and pass
quietly to all liberal and refining arts and occupations. This
is clear, from the instances of the eminent monarchies of the
East—Meroe, Thebes, Memphis, Babylon, Nineveh, Bagdad,
and Mosul. So, too, on the Indus and Ganges, in the provinces
of Taxila, Maghada, Benares ; or later, in the great empire
whose centres were Agra and Delhi. China has arrived at its
highest civilisation in the fertile district between its two
greatest rivers."—Ritter, *Comp. Geography*, Gage's Trans. 183.

[1] Berosus, Cory's *Ancient Fragments*, 22.
[2] The Euphrates and Tigris "run through Media and Pare-
tacena ; into Mesopotamia, which, from its lying in the middle
between these two rivers, has gained from them that name."—
Diod. Sic. ii. 1.

In the plain or "field" of the Euphrates (called Edinna, Eden, in the ancient Accadian tongue) the Bible legend places the first beginnings of all rivers, and the *planting* of that first *garden, in the midst of* which grew the *tree of life.* There men first lived, and invented the arts; there the lines of civilisation were first laid down.

SACRED TREE FROM AN EARLY BABYLONIAN CYLINDER.

There Oannes, the great Fish-god, appearing out of "the Erythraean sea, which borders upon Babylonia," taught to men "letters and sciences and arts of every kind," so that no great discovery has ever been made since.[1] And there

---

[1] Berosus, in Cory's *Fragments,* 23.—Berosus, a Babylonian, belonged to the learned class or caste, whom the Greeks called Chaldeans and regarded as priests. He lived at the time of Alexander's conquests, and is supposed to have written the history of his country in the Greek language for the enlightenment of her new masters. "As a priest of Belus," says Cory, "he possessed every advantage which the

took place that Flood which has left its mark on the literature of many lands.

OANNES (EA) FROM NIMROUD SCULPTURE.
After Rawlinson (Murray).

In the 11th Tablet of the Gisdhubar series,[1] the great Epic of Early Chaldea, which is the Semitic translation of an Accadian original dating from 2000 B.C. or earlier, Xisuthrus, the Chaldean Noah, relates to his son Gisdhubar (the hunter, leader, records of the Temple and the learning and traditions of the Chaldeans could afford." Extracts from his work have been preserved by Apollodorus and others—how far faithfully is uncertain.

[1] Discovered by Mr. Smith in 1872. — Smith, *Babylonia*, 25 ; Sayce and Smith, *Chaldean Genesis*, 175, 178, 202. The translation of the legend has been kindly corrected for me by Mr. Pinches of the British Museum, to whom I owe grateful thanks for much kindly help.

and king, who is often identified with the Biblical Nimrod) the story of the Flood.

" The city of Surippak," he says, " the city which thou knowest, lies on the Euphrates, this city was already ancient when the gods within it set their hearts to bring on a deluge. . . . Ea, the lord of wisdom, sat among them, and repeated their decree to the earth . . . O man of Surippak . . . (The gods) will destroy the hostile and save life, —cause the seed of life of every kind to mount into the midst of the ship, the ship which thou shalt build. . . . [Enter and turn the door of the ship, bring into the midst of it thy corn, thy property, and thy goods, thy (family), thy household, thy relatives, and the sons of the people. The (cattle) of the field, the wild beasts of the field, as many as I would preserve, I will send unto thee.] . . . The season Samas fixed, and he spake, saying, 'In the night will I cause the heaven to rain destruction. Enter into the midst of the ship and shut thy door.' . . . Then Mu-seri-ina-namari (the water of Dawn at daylight) arose from the horizon of heaven like a black cloud. Rimmon in the midst of it thundered; Nebo and Lugal (the king) went in front; the throne-bearers (the seven

wicked spirits or storm-gods) go over mountain
and plain; Nergal the mighty removes the wicked;
Adar goes overthrowing all before him.   The
spirits of earth carried the flood; in their terrible-
ness they sweep through the land; the deluge
of Rimmon reaches unto Heaven; all that was
light to [darkness] was turned.   (The surface)
of the land like (fire?) they wasted; swiftly
they swept . . . like battle against men they
came. . . ."

Most of the details—even to the dove which
went and returned, finding *no resting-place*, and
the raven which *did not return*—and some of
the very words and phrases found in the Biblical,
are also found in the cuneiform account; while
certain curious differences between them can
be traced to the fact that the Hebrews were
an inland and not a sea-going people.   Thus
they call their vessel a "coffer," not (like the
Accadians) a ship; and in Genesis nothing is
said about testing its seaworthiness, or providing
a pilot.

On one main point, the cuneiform and Biblical
accounts are agreed, and herein they differ from
the other traditions of the deluge found through-

out the world—namely, in representing the Flood
to have been sent as a punishment for the wickedness of men. No such moral cause appears in
the legends of other lands.

The Accadians are the first dwellers in Mesopotamia of whom we have any definite knowledge.
Their inscriptions, stamped on bricks—the wonderful cuneiform or wedge-shaped writing which they
had invented,—show that they were a flourishing and civilised people more than 2000 years
before the Christian era. Some suppose that
they belonged to the Hamitic race,—that they
were dark-skinned *sons of Ham* like the
Egyptians; but we do not know with any
certainty to which of the great races of men they
in truth belonged. We only know that they were
the creators of a civilisation perhaps not less
ancient, and certainly not less wonderful, than
that of Egypt,—of a civilisation which has had a
far deeper and wider influence upon the history of
the world than has the Egyptian.

For to these ancient Accadian dwellers in the
plain of the Euphrates, we can trace back the first
beginnings of arithmetic, of geometry, and of

astronomy.[1] They compiled the calendar; they
gave the names of the seven planets to the seven
days of the week; they instituted the Sabbath.[2]
Their divisions of time are those which to-day are
still recognised among all the civilised peoples of
the world. They understood the wonderful art of
writing, and their language continued to be the
language of science and learning even in the
latest times of the Semitic Casdim, or conquerors.
They had flourishing cities — *Babel, and Erech,
and Accad, and Calneh* (Gen. x. 10)—with stately
palaces and temples. They had *brick for stone*

---

[1] Simplicius relates that Callisthenes, the friend of Alexander,
sent to Aristotle from Babylon a series of stellar observations,
reaching back 1903 years before the taking of Babylon by
Alexander (1903 + 331 = 2234 B.C.). — Smith and Sayce, *Ch.
Genesis*, 199. See Loftus, *Chaldea and Susiana*, 32 ; G. Rawlinson, *Five Great Monarchies*, i. 101.

[2] "There can be no doubt that the Sabbath was an Accadian
institution. The Accadian words by which the idea is denoted
literally mean 'a day on which work is unlawful,' and are
interpreted in the bilingual tablets as signifying 'a day of
peace,' or 'completion of labours.'" The calendar lays down
the following injunctions to the king (the "prince of many
nations," literally *shepherd*) for each of these Sabbaths :
" . . . Sacrifice he may not offer. The king may not ride in
his chariot. In royal fashion he may not legislate. A review of
the army the general may not hold. Medicine for his sickness
of body he may not apply."—Smith and Sayce, *Ch. Genesis*,
89. See Renan, *Hist.* i. 68.

in that country of the plain, and "*slime*" (bitumen) *had they for mortar* (xi. 3); and their huge buildings, whose tops *reached unto heaven*, living in the horrified remembrance of the simple pastoral people who came to dwell among them, as gigantic monuments of folly, have formed the basis of the legend of the Tower of Babel, which has been handed down to our own day.[1]

The man *par excellence*, the special human being made by the Creator—Adamu, "the man,"

---

[1] Mr. Smith discovered a fragment of the Babylonian version of the story, and it is interesting to find that in this the very same word (signifying "to confound") is used as in the Hebrew account. The Hebrew writer once, too (Gen. xi. 7), " adopts the polytheistic language of the Accadian scribe ; the Lord being made to say, ' Let *us* go down and there confound their language.' " But the derivation of Babel from *Balbel*, "to confound" (Gen. xi. 9), is one of those plays on words of which the Old Testament writers are so fond, Babel being *Bab-Ili*, " the gate of God," which was the Semitic translation of an old Accadian name with the same meaning (*Ch. Genesis*, 166-168). " In order to render their edifices more durable the Babylonians submitted them, when erected, to the heat of a furnace. This will account for the remarkable condition of the brickwork on the summit of the Birs Nimrúd, which has undoubtedly been subjected to the agency of fire. No wonder that the early explorers, carried away by their feelings of reverence, should have ascribed the vitrified and molten aspect of the ruins to the avenging fire of heaven."— Loftus, *Chaldea and Susiana*, p. 31.

—belonged to the dark-skinned race of Accad, the aboriginal population of Babylonia, who in the inscriptions of Nebuchadnezzar are still called Blackheads (*Rec.* iii. N. S. 153).

In the sixth century before our era, Nabonidus, digging among the foundations of the Sun-god's temple at Babylon, discovered the "foundation-stone of Naram Sin, the son of Sargon, which for three thousand two hundred years no king going before ever had seen." On these data, then, 3800 B.C. is about the time when Babylonian history, as known to us, may be said to begin. But after Sargon of Accad and his son, one of the earliest kings whose inscriptions have come down to us is Ur-Bau, who seems to have ruled in Ur of the Chaldees[1] about the thirtieth century before Christ. He is sometimes identified

---

[1] It is probable that Ur of the Chaldees is "Ur of the Casdim," Casdim being an Assyrian word meaning conquerors, which might be applied to the Semitic tribe after their conquest of Babylonia. The Greek names Chaldean and Chaldea are derived from "the Kaldai, a small tribe settled on the Persian Gulf and first mentioned in the ninth century B.C., who, under Merodach-Baladan (B.C. 721–709), possessed themselves of Babylonia, and became so integral a portion of its inhabitants as to give their name to the whole of them in classical times."—Smith and Sayce, *Ch. Genesis*, 318.

with the Orchamus of Ovid, and is supposed to
have been of the family of the mythical Nimrod,
son of Cush, the son of Ham, the *mighty hunter
before the Lord,* who (tradition says) was ruler over
Ur at the time of Abraham, and who, according
to Josephus, "tyrannised at Babylon" (i. 6, 2).

SIGNET CYLINDER OF KING UR-BAU.—After Rawlinson (Murray).

In the days of Ur-Bau the country was already
at a high stage of civilisation, as is proved by the
many works on geography, astronomy, and other
sciences among the tablets found in the ancient
"library" at Ur, and by the beautifully-engraved
seals of the time.

But Ur-Bau evidently marks an epoch in the life of the nation, and he seems to have been the mightiest constructor and conqueror who ruled in Babylonia before the time of Nebuchadnezzar.

The great temple at Ur (literally The City) was the work of his reign, and on the bricks among its ruins may still be seen his inscriptions. The temple was dedicated to Nannar, the Moon-god, "Lord of Building," "Protector of the Land," who had precedence in the Babylonian mythology, as so often among desert tribes, over his offspring Samas, fierce Sun-god, he whose hot breath destroyed their crops and dried up their streams.

"To Nannar, eldest son of Bel his king," says an inscription, "Ur-Bau the powerful man, lord of Erech, king of Ur, king of Sumir and Akkad, Ê-te-im-ila, his beloved Temple, he has built, he has restored its site."

Ur is now called Mugheir, or Mukeyyer, the "place of bitumen." In the centuries that have gone by the river-course has changed, and by the silting up of the end of the Persian Gulf, the boundary between sea and land advances seawards year by year; so that the Mugheir of to-day lies some miles from the river-bank, and far from the mud-flats of the shore.[1] But in the time of Ur-Bau the city probably commanded, not only

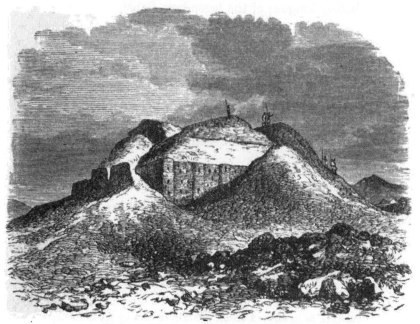

RUINS AT MUGHEIR.—After Rawlinson (Murray).

the great rivers which were the highway of commerce, but also the sea, and thus was one of the

[1] Speaking of the increase of land at the delta of the Tigris and Euphrates, Loftus (*Chaldea and Susiana*, 282) says : "Since the commencement of our era there has been an increment at the extraordinary rate of a mile in about seventy years, which far exceeds the growth of any existing delta. This rapid increase is accounted for by the deposit of the river mud in the confined

marts of the world, a port where many nations and languages would meet—the character of that busy region being, no doubt, typified in the conflicting tongues of the legendary Babel.

To Babylonia had come wandering from Arabia (then far more fertile than it is to-day) a shepherd tribe of the race which it has been agreed to call "Semitic," the children of Shem.[1] First as settlers, then as supplanters, they came among the Accadians; and, in the city of the Moon-god, lived (probably during the time of Dungi, son of Ur-Bau) Abram, or Abraham, son of Terah, of the *generations of Shem*.

The name of Abraham finds no place upon the monuments, or in the records of the Accadian kings; but the Semitic traditions about him are many.

basin of the gulf, where, instead of being washed away by currents, as in an open ocean, it is driven back by the returning tide." See also Fraser, *Mesopotamia*, 148.

[1] Renan in his *Histoire des Langues Sémitiques*, 2, suggests that a better name for the group would be "Syro-arabes," the meaning of Gen. x. being "géographique, et nullement ethnographique." "Du reste," he adds, "la dénomination de Sémitiques ne peut avoir d'inconvénient, du moment qu'on la prend comme une simple appellation conventionnelle, et que l'on s'est expliqué sur ce qu'elle renferme de profondément inexact." See also Kenrick's *Phoenicia*, 49, "Colour, and not language, was the principle of classification."

"Berosus mentions our Father Abram, without naming him," says Josephus, "when he says thus :—' In the tenth generation after the Flood, there was among the Chaldeans a man righteous and great, and skilful in the celestial science'" (i. 7, 2).

It is said that *Terah the father of Abraham* not only *served other gods* (Josh. xxiv. 2), but that he was himself a maker of idols [1]—idols, perhaps, of Il or Ra, the remote and mysterious deity who,

"High throned above all highth,"

was at the head of the Babylonian Pantheon ; and of Anu and Bel and Hea ; of Samas and Nannar ; of Nergal the king of battles, whose symbol was the great man-lion ; and of "Istar the queen," the only feminine divinity whom the Accadians recognised, and who as *Ashtoreth, the goddess of the Zidonians* (1 Kings xi.), became the prototype of the Grecian Aphrodite.

The tradition preserved in the Koran says that

[1] The worship of idols characterises a somewhat higher stage of human development than that of the mere savage. "It may, I think," says Sir J. Lubbock, "be laid down almost as a constant rule, that mankind arrives at the stage of monarchy in government before he reaches idolatry in religion."—*Origin of Civilisation*, p. 259.

Abraham provoked a conflict with the people of the land, because, in his scorn of this idol-worship, he broke their images in pieces. " He broke them all in pieces, except the chief of them, that to it they might return." " He went aside to their gods and said, Do ye not eat ? What aileth you that ye do not speak ? He broke out upon them, with the right hand striking."

Another tradition in the Koran tells that he was made to pass his youth in a cave, and that when he first emerged and " the night over-shadowed him, he beheld a star. 'This,' said he, ' is my Lord': but when it set, he said, ' I love not gods which set.' And when he beheld the moon uprising, ' This,' said he, ' is my Lord': but when it set, he said, ' Surely if my Lord guide me not, I shall surely be of those who go astray.' And when he beheld the sun uprise, he said, ' This is my Lord ; this is greatest.' But when it set, he said, ' O my people ! I share not with you the guilt of joining gods with God; I turn my face to him who hath created the Heavens and the Earth, following the right religion : I am not one of those who add gods to God.' And his people disputed with him."

"He was," says Josephus, "the first that ventured to publish this notion, that there was but one God, the Creator of the universe . . . to whom alone we ought justly to offer our honour and thanksgiving. For which doctrines, when the Chaldeans and other people of Mesopotamia raised a tumult against him, he thought fit to leave that country" (i. 7, 1).

He and his people, so it is written in the book of Judith, "would not follow the gods of their fathers, which were in the land of Chaldea. For they left the way of their ancestors, and worshipped the God of heaven, the God whom they knew: so they cast them out from the face of their gods, and they fled" (v. 7, 8).

It may be that this enlightenment of faith constituted the "call" of Abraham. In any case, we read that he and his family went forth, *and Terah took Abram his son, and Lot the son of Haran his son's son, and Sarai his daughter-in-law, his son Abram's wife; and they went forth with them from Ur of the Chaldees, to go into the land of Canaan; and they came unto Haran*—the frontier fortress of the Babylonian empire, whose

C

name signified "the road"—*and dwelt there* (Gen. xi. 31).

Thus did Abraham take to that wandering shepherd life that, even more than the "bon sens précoce" which Renan sees in all Semitic nations, preserved his race from idolatry. "Le désert est monothéiste."

We may imagine the caravan travelling slowly up the river, along causeways raised high above the network of canals, past cities and groves of palms and pleasant gardens, rising like islands "from a golden sea of waving corn,"[1] past the bitumen springs of Hit, where the dead flat of the alluvial plain changes to a rolling upland, watered by many mountain streams.

And they came unto Haran and dwelt there (Gen. xi. 31). The fertile valleys of Upper Mesopotamia became the headquarters of Abraham's tribe. Thither he sent, long years after he himself had wandered onwards, to take a wife unto his son Isaac, from his *father's house and from his kindred* (xxiv.). There was the spot where his servant *made his camels to kneel down*

[1] Loftus, *Chaldea and Susiana*, 14. See also Fraser, *Mesopotamia*, 26.

without the city by a well of water at the time of the evening, even the time that women go out to draw water (xxiv. 11); and there the *land of the people of the east* where, later, Rachel *kept her father's sheep,* and where Jacob served those seven years which *seemed unto him but a few days, for the love he had to her* (xxix.).

In this land of wells and pastures Abraham sojourned some time, *and Terah died in Haran.* But at last the day came when he started again upon his wanderings, when the broad Euphrates lay behind him, and he became "the Hebrew, the man who had crossed the river flood," the foreigner from beyond the water.

"The outward appearances which, in the case of the Greeks and Romans, we know only through art and writing, through marble, fresco, and parchment," says Dean Stanley in a well-known passage, "in the case of Jewish history we know through the forms of actual men, living and moving before us, wearing almost the same garb, speaking in almost the same language, and certainly with the same general turns of speech and tone and manners. Such as we see them now, starting on a pilgrimage or a journey, were

Abraham and his brother's son, when they ' went forth' to go into the land of Canaan. 'All their substance that they had "gathered"' is heaped high on the backs of their kneeling camels. The 'slaves that they had bought in Haran' run along by their sides. Round about them are their flocks of sheep and goats, and the asses moving underneath the towering forms of the camels. The chief is there, amidst the stir of movement, or resting at noon within his black tent, marked out from the rest by his cloak of brilliant scarlet, by the fillet of rope which binds the loose handkerchief round his head, by the spear which he holds in his hand to guide the march, and to fix the encampment. The chief's wife, the Princess of the tribe, is there in her own tent to make the cakes and prepare the usual meal of milk and butter ; the slave or the child is ready to bring in the red lentil soup for the weary hunter, or to kill the calf for the unexpected guest. Even the ordinary social state is the same : polygamy, slavery, the exclusiveness of family ties ; the period of service for the dowry of a wife ; the solemn obligations of hospitality ; the temptations, easily followed, into craft or falsehood " (i. 9).

So Abram departed, as the Lord had spoken unto him . . . and Abram took Sarai his wife, and Lot his brother's son, and all their substance that they had gathered, and the souls that they had gotten in Haran; and they went forth to go into the land of Canaan; and into the land of Canaan they came. And Abram passed through the land unto the place of Sichem, unto the plain of Moreh. And the Canaanite was then in the land (Gen. xii. 4-6).

These Canaanites, though so radically differing in character and religion from the later Jews, belonged to the same great family of men as did Abraham. Neither their language nor their customs would be altogether strange to the Hebrew newcomer. For this people—of whom we hear so much in later history under their Greek name of Phoenicians [1]—were a branch of the same Semitic race from Arabia who had settled in Babylonia; and the mysterious Melchizedek,

---

[1] Genesis x. 6 makes Canaan one of the *sons of Ham*; but the community of language between the Hebrews and the Phoenicians must be taken as settling the question of their common origin. Hatred of the Canaanites caused the later Jews to affiliate Canaan to Ham, for whose sin he was *cursed* and made the *servant of Shem* (Gen. ix. 25). Renan, i. 96.

king of Salem, priest of the most high God, who met Abraham returning from the slaughter of the kings, and blessed him (Heb. vii. 1), was, according to Jewish traditions, Shem the son of Noah himself.

Through Canaan Abraham wandered with his caravan. Where food was plentiful he pitched his tent and fed his cattle; when it failed, he *removed* (lit. *plucked up* his tent pegs), and journeyed onwards to find fresh pastures, *going on still toward the south.*

Then at last there came upon the inhabitants of Canaan one of those droughts to which their country has always been subject.

And there was a famine in the land: and Abram went down into Egypt to sojourn there; for the famine was grievous in the land.

Abraham is thus the first recorded of myriad travellers who have crossed the "bridge of nations," the first of that long series of Semitic wanderers who *saw that there was corn in Egypt* (Gen. xlii. 1), and came *down* from their own parched highlands, when the *rain of heaven* failed them, to take refuge in a country which did not depend upon local rainfall, a land which was watered with the foot, *as a garden of herbs.*[1]

Egypt, it has been well said, "is the background of the whole history of the Israelites." It "is to them the land of plenty, whilst the neighbouring nations starve; its long strip of garden-land was the oasis of the primitive world."[2] Herodotus calls it "an acquired country, the gift of the River" Nile. He says of the dwellers in its delta: "At present it must be confessed they obtain the fruits of the field with less trouble than any other people in the world," since the husbandman has but to wait "till the river has, of its own accord, spread itself over the fields and withdrawn again to its bed, and then sows his plot of ground, and after sowing turns his swine into it—the swine tread in the corn—afterwhich he has only to await the harvest" (ii. 14).

---

[1] "*For the land, whither thou goest in to possess it, is not as the land of Egypt, from whence ye came out, where thou sowedst thy seed, and wateredst it with thy foot, as a garden of herbs: but the land, whither ye go to possess it, is a land of hills and valleys, and drinketh water of the rain of heaven*" (Deut. xi. 10, 11). In the plenteous years in Egypt "*Joseph gathered corn as the sand of the sea, very much, until he left numbering; for it was without number*" (Gen. xli. 49).

[2] Stanley, *Sinai and Palestine*, Introduction.

Here, in this second home of plenty, the
wanderer from the far-off cities of Babylonia, the
Hebrew from beyond the Euphrates, came in
contact with another of the great early civilisations
of the world. We have no means of knowing
when this contact took place : authorities differ as
to the earlier dates in Egyptian history by some
two thousand years ; but there can be no question
that the civilisation of Egypt was not only well
established, but ancient, in the days of Abraham.
Of Menes, the mythical lawgiver, whom all early
authorities agree in describing as the first mortal
king of Egypt, there are no contemporary monuments or records. The great Dyke, which turned
aside the river Nile from its former bed, where
Memphis now stands,—that work of skill which
" meets us on the threshold of Egyptian history," [1]

[1] S. Poole, *Cities of Egypt*, 21

" After the gods," says Diodorus (Cory's *Fragments*, 150),
" Menas was the first king of the Egyptians," and this is one of
the few points upon which all the early authorities—Herodotus,
Eratosthenes, Diodorus, Manetho — agree (see Cory's *Fragments*). But, as Mr. Rawlinson has pointed out, " a name like
that of Menes is found at the beginning of things in so many
nations, that on that account alone the word would be suspi-
cious : in Greece it is Minos, in Phrygia Manis, in Lydia Manes,
in India Menes, in Germany Manus" (Rawlinson, *Egypt*, 53).

—is supposed to have been his. And it has been suggested also that we should not be far wrong if we ventured to ascribe the great Sphinx of Ghizeh, the most ancient statue known, either to him or to the generations before him, called in the priestly chronicles the "Servants of Horus." [1] The Sphinx was certainly in existence in the time of the Pyramid - builders, Cheops and Chephren and Mycerinus, and these monarchs certainly lived and died many centuries before any date at which we can place Abraham.

The Pyramids—those

> "memorials
> Of the great unremembered, that can show
> The mass and shape they wore four thousand years ago"—

probably stood round about Memphis in the days of Abraham even as they stand to-day. Nay, their construction was probably already a matter of legend. Abraham may well have been told the same traditions as were told to the Greeks, so many centuries later, of the cruel oppression by means of which those gigantic monuments— "greatest of the world's sepulchres"—were reared. Mycerinus, says Diodorus, "detesting the severity

---

[1] Maspéro, *Eg. Arch.* 20.

of the former kings, carried himself all his days gently and graciously towards all his subjects" (i. 5), and the oracle cut short his years. Cheops and Chephren, on the other hand, have taken their place in literature[1] as kings who

". . . loved injustice and lived long."

"It took ten years' oppression of the people to make a causeway for the conveyance of the stones" for the great Pyramid, says Herodotus, and 100,000 men laboured constantly at the Pyramid itself for twenty years, during which Cheops "closed the temples, and forbade the Egyptians to offer sacrifice, compelling them instead to labour, one and all, in his service" (ii. 124).

SIGNET OF CHEOPS.

But, as a matter of fact, in the inscriptions on the monuments of the Pyramid period we

---

[1] "The monuments must be consulted, that we may know what the history of Egypt was; the Greek writers, that we may know what the world has till lately believed it to be."— Kenrick, *Ancient Egypt*, ii. 87.

Herodotus was born in a Greek colony of Asia Minor in 484 B.C.—that is to say, soon after Marathon and before Thermopylae and Salamis. He not only explored Egypt, but travelled much in Greece and Asia Minor, and visited both

see no evidence of such oppression, nor of a barbarous or primitive state of society. Not only "the construction of the Pyramids, but the scenes depicted in the sculptured tombs of this epoch, show that the Egyptians had already the same habits and arts as in after times. . . . We see no primitive mode of life; no barbarous customs; not even the habit, so slowly abandoned by all people, of wearing arms when not on military service; nor any archaic art." [1]

We see the civilisation of Egypt, on the contrary, as highly organised, with every appearance of an existence as ancient, as at the time of the invasions of Cambyses or of Alexander. We see the great lords of Egypt dwelling each among his

---

Tyre and Babylon. Diodorus (who visited Egypt about 58 B.C.) is further removed from the events he describes, and is also a far less reliable witness. He takes occasion, however, to be very severe on Herodotus, as belonging to those writers of Egyptian history "who wilfully pursue and prefer prodigious stories before truth, and relate a company of fictions merely for sport and diversion sake" (i. 6).

Herodotus and Diodorus are both very misleading as to chronology and the sequence of events. Herodotus, for instance, places the Pyramids after the time of Rameses, "which is very much like placing Charlemagne after Louis XIV." (Mariette, *Monuments of Upper Egypt*, 13), only more so.

[1] Sir G. Wilkinson in Rawlinson's *Herodotus*, ii. 343.

own people, with the pride of a patriarch in the train of slaves and in the household of artisans who formed his "family" and lived under his not unkindly rule. His house and furniture were beautiful, refined, and costly; his way of living was "delicate and sumptuous" (D. i. 4). An inscription of the Pyramid period records the offerings of images of stone, gold, bronze, ivory, and ebony to the gods. The sepulchre of Chufu (Cheops) was called the "Splendour of Pyramids": it is even said that the art of his period was better, inasmuch as it was far more lifelike and less conventional, than that of later times.

And such as the civilisation of Egypt was during the period of the Pyramid-builders, such does it seem to have been during the xIIth dynasty, the Usertesens and Amenemhats, under whose rule it is supposed that Abraham may have visited the country, and whose era is certainly one of the most brilliant of Egyptian history. "In the tombs of the Pyramid period are represented the same fowling and fishing scenes as occur later; the rearing of cattle and wild animals of the desert; the scribes using the same kind of reed, for writing on the papyrus an inventory of the

estate which was to be presented to the owner;
the same boats" (Egypt was then, as in the time
of the prophets, a "*land shadowing with wings*,"
Is. xviii. 1)—". . . the same mode of preparing
for the entertainment of guests; the same introduction of music and dancing; the same trades,
as glass-blowers, cabinetmakers, and others; as
well as similar agricultural scenes, implements,
and granaries."[1]

Upon the entrance wall of the great tomb of
Khnum-hotep, Governor of the Eastern Provinces,
at Benihassan, there is a most interesting epitaph
upon one of his ancestors, another high official of
the same noble family, named Ameni, who died in
the forty-third year of Usertesen I., and whose recorded virtues supply good proof, if not of his
own attainment, at least of the social standard of
his day.

"No little child have I injured," he says; "no
widow have I oppressed; no fisherman have I
hindered; no shepherd have I detained. . . .
There was no poverty in my days, no starvation
in my time when there were years of famine. I
ploughed all the fields of Mah to its southern and

[1] Sir G. Wilkinson in Rawlinson's *Herodotus*, ii. 343.

northern frontiers. I gave life to its inhabitants, making its food; no one was starved in it. I gave to the widow as to the married woman. I made no difference between the Great and the Little, in all that I did. When the Nile made a great inundation, I did not take out of the fields." [1]

Of the inscription to Khnum-hotep himself, who was made governor under Amenemhat II., Brugsch, writing in 1859, says : "L'auteur égyptien qui l'a composée, nous y fait reconnaître l'heureux temps d'un sage et paisible gouvernement, plein de zèle pour le bien de ses sujets, pour le souvenir des ·morts, et pour le service religieux des dieux. Dans les mêmes endroits où, de nos jours, de pauvres villages habités par une misérable population se présentent aux yeux du voyageur attristé, il y avait jadis des champs cultivés et arrosés par une multitude de canaux; des villes florissantes, habitées par une population gaie et laborieuse." [2]

There are upon the walls, alike of the Pyramids and of the rock-hewn tombs at Benihassan, pictures representing every phase of the daily life

---

[1] *Rec.* xii. 63. See also Epitaph of Khnum-hotep, son of Nehera, himself (Brugsch, *Hist.* i. 59).

[2] *Hist. d'Egypte*, i. 59.

of those periods : we see the family, the father, head of the household, at table or at the chase, with his wife, always his equal and companion (not, as with uncivilised nations, his slave or inferior). We see his children and dependants at their daily labour in field and vineyard and workshop ;[1] or in their games—hunting, wrestling, playing on musical instruments, or dancing, always apparently gay, agile, and content.

The pleasant picture hardly varies with the centuries, in these early times ; and thus, although we do not know within many hundred years when it was that Abraham visited the country, yet we can form a fairly good idea of what the Egypt he looked upon was like.

" The extraordinary clearness and dryness of the

---

[1] We find a curious description of the trades then practised in Egypt, from the point of view of the hardships which attended them, in a letter of instruction, " In praise of learning," addressed by "a person of Tsaru " (? Tanis) to his son Pepi (in the XIIth or possibly VIth dynasty, but copied later). He goes into minute particulars concerning the hardships incident to every trade—labourers, blacksmiths, stonecutters, barbers, boatmen, builders, gardeners, farmers, makers of weapons, couriers, sandalmakers, washermen, "fathers of waters," fowlers, fishermen—and concludes with the advice, "Consider, there is not an employment destitute of superior ones, except the scribe." *Rec.* viii. 147.

climate ; the rare circumstance of the vicinity of the desert sands which have preserved what they have overwhelmed ; the passionate desire of the old Egyptians to perpetuate every familiar and loved object as long as human power and skill could reach, have all contributed to this result. The wars, the amusements, the meals, the employments, the portraits, nay, even the very bodies, of those ancient fathers of the civilised world are still among us. We can form a clearer image of the court of the Pharaohs, in all external matters, than we can of the court of Augustus." And if this was true when Dean Stanley wrote these words, still more is it true to-day, when the discoveries of Deir-el-bahari have enabled us to gaze upon the very features of the royal dead, and to learn more than we ever knew before of their habit as they lived.

Usertesen I., of the xiith dynasty, is the earliest known of the great Egyptian conquerors. He subdued Cush or Ethiopia, and he left memorials of his power in Nubia and in Sinai, as well as in every city of ancient Egypt. Though afterwards confounded with the great kings of the xixth dynasty, he seems to have been the original Sesostris of the Greeks ; and his architectural works were as remarkable as his conquests. The greatest of these was the Temple of the Sun at Heliopolis. Usertesen's Obelisk — the oldest known in Egypt, and therefore in the world— stands to-day on the wide green plain, as it probably stood in the days of Abraham, a "petrified sunbeam," whose slender shaft of pink granite, pointing upwards, catches the sun's earliest and latest rays.

Little else now remains of the ancient city where the father-in-law of Joseph was priest; where Moses became *learned in all the wisdom of the Egyptians* (Acts vii. 22); where Herodotus collected his materials, because the priests were "the best skilled in history of all the Egyptians" (ii. 3); and where, in the time of Strabo, was still shown the house in which Plato had studied. The city of the sun was destroyed by the Persian Cambyses : then was done according to the word of Jeremiah, "*He shall break also the images of Bethshemesh* (the house of the sun), *that is in the land of Egypt ; and the houses of the gods of the Egyptians shall he burn with fire*" (xliii. 13).

Another great monarch of the XIIth dynasty was Amenemhat III., named by the Greeks Moeris, "the Beloved," who built the Labyrinth, and made the great reservoir, "one of the most stupendous works of the old Empire,"[1] to regulate the yearly overflow of the Nile, upon which depended the well-being of the whole country. Amenemhat III. was worshipped as a god by the kings of the XVIIIth dynasty; and it may be that he was the monarch with whom Abraham came into contact, when the princes of the Pharaoh [2] saw Sarai his wife, and *commended her before Pharaoh* because she was *very fair* (Gen. xii.).

There is naturally no special inscription upon the monuments which can date an event so unimportant to a Pharaoh of Egypt as the advent of a Bedouin chief to seek food in his dominions. "On ne bavarde pas," says Renan, "sur la pierre et le métal." But there is upon the wall of the

[1] Birch, *Egypt*, 7. But "I no longer believe that Lake Moeris ever existed," says another great authority (Maspéro, *Eg. Arch.* 36).

[2] It used to be thought that Pharaoh meant "child of the sun"; but the name is now believed to be derived from Peraa or Perao, "the great house," like the Turkish Porte. Pharaoh was, of course, not the name of any individual king, but the title of all Egyptian kings, like the Russian Czar; or the name of an office, as the term Rabshakeh is used in 2 Kings and in Isaiah. Shishak, who lived in the time of Solomon, is the first Pharaoh of Egypt who is spoken of by name, in the Bible.

great tomb at Benihassan, already referred to, a sculpture in which certain Semitic foreigners are represented as arriving, just as Abraham might have arrived, at the court of the governor Khnum-hotep. Their dress and arms show the party to be foreigners, and they are being ushered into the presence of the great lord, with their women, their children (seated in panniers on an ass's back), and their offerings ; while a scribe unfolds a roll on which it is recorded that they are Amu or Semites, coming before the chief with an offering of the stibium or antimony, which the Egyptians used to blacken the skin beneath their eyes.

The chief, towering above the suppliant party, is receiving them graciously ; and we may fancy that he will *entreat them well,* as the Pharaoh did Abraham, and that they will have *sheep, and oxen, and he-asses, and men-servants, and maid-servants, and she - asses, and camels,* so that they may return, as did Abraham, *very rich in cattle, in silver, and in gold.*

Finally, after his sojourn in Egypt, the story of Abraham takes us back to the Land of Promise, where were passed the last scenes of his long life. *And Abraham went up out of Egypt* (Gen. xiii. 1), *and dwelt in the land of Canaan.*

It is now that Scripture history first brings before us those *children of Heth,* or Hittites, who played so large, though, until lately, so mysterious, a part in the history of the Chosen People. They were the outposts of the great Hittite empire which we now know to have at one time ruled from the banks of the Euphrates to the shores of the Aegean Sea; they belonged to "that long-forgotten but wonderful race, whose restoration to history has been one of the most curious discoveries of the present age."

To us the Hittites are deeply interesting—not only because their "resurrection" confirms many details in Scripture history which have hitherto been the prey of the commentator—"not alone because of the influence they once exercised on the fortunes of the Chosen People, not alone because a Hittite was the wife of David and the ancestress of Christ, but also on account of the debt which the civilisation of our own Europe owes to them. Our culture is the inheritance we have received from Ancient Greece, and the first beginnings of Greek culture were derived from the Hittite conquerors of Asia Minor. The Hittite warriors who still guard the Pass of Karabel, on the very threshold of Asia, are symbols of the position occupied by the race in the education of mankind. The Hittites carried the time-worn civilisations of Babylonia and Egypt to the farthest boundary of Asia, and then handed them over to the west, in the gray dawn of European history." [1]

We are startled when we come upon evidences

[1] Sayce, *Hittites*, 121. See also 66, 142.

Dr. Wright has given us an amusing account of the rescue of the first known relics of Hittite literature at Hamath in 1872. A meteoric shower in the night followed their removal, and the inhabitants sent a deputation to the Waly "to tell him of the evil omens and to urge a restoration of the stones. The Waly ordered coffee and cigarettes for all the members of the deputation, who squatted in solemn dignity around him. He listened patiently to all the speakers, several of whom spoke at great length and with much animation. When they had finished the Waly continued stroking his beard for some time. Then he asked, in a very grave manner, if the stars had hurt any one. They replied they had not. 'Ah,' said the Waly, brightening up and speaking with a cheery ringing voice that even the guards outside the door might hear, 'the omens were good. They indicated the shining approbation of Allah on your loyalty in sending these precious stones to your beloved Khalif, the Father of the Faithful.' The grave deputation rose up comforted. Each member kissed the Waly's hand and withdrew." —*Empire of the Hittites*, 10.

of this long-forgotten race, enshrined in Greek mythology—such as the weeping Niobe of Sipylos, which was the image of a Hittite goddess graven on the dripping limestone rock; or the Amazons, who were the armed priestesses of the great goddess of Asia Minor, the prototype of the Ephesian Diana; —when we read that the great two-headed eagle, the emblem of the Russian and Austrian emperors of to-day, was the sign and symbol of Hittite art, adopted in later days by the Turkoman princes, and carried by the Crusaders to Europe in the fourteenth century.

There is much in the Mongolian or Chinese-like appearance of the Hittites upon their monuments which reminds us of the Babylonian Accadians — the Blackheads of later inscriptions; their language is a Mongol dialect, closely akin to the Accadian, and their religion was undoubtedly borrowed from Babylonia. But they seem to have descended into Syria from the snow-clad slopes of the Taurus; and the snow-shoes with upturned ends, the long fingerless gloves, with which they are always represented on their monuments, bear witness to their having come from the cold regions of the north.

Whatever their origin, the Hittites had been a distinct people before the earliest dawn of history —long before Abraham went forth from Ur; and there are inscriptions which tell of their conflicts with Sargon of Accad as early as the year 3800 B.C.

It may well have been with them that *Abram the Hebrew* joined in repelling the invasion of the four Accadian kings (Gen. xiv.). There was evidently no hostility as yet between the Hebrews and the races already established in Canaan. But Abraham is represented as being ever a *stranger and a sojourner* with them (xxiii. 4); and we are expressly told that when he *stood up from before his dead,* and asked from Ephron the Hittite that burying-place which is "the one fixed element in the unstable life of a nomadic race," he refused to take it as a gift, but insisted on weighing out to the children of Heth *four hundred shekels of silver, current money with the merchant* (xxiii. 16).[1]

---

[1] The story of the purchase, still told among the modern Arabs of Hebron, is a counterpart of the legendary stratagem by which a Semite of other days, the Phoenician Dido, obtained land enough for Byrsa, the citadel of Carthage. "Ibrahim asked only as much ground as could be covered with a cow's

Thus did he acquire *Machpelah, before Mamre: the same is Hebron in the land of Canaan.   And the field, and the cave that is therein, were made sure unto Abraham, for a possession of a burying-place, by the sons of Heth* (Gen. xxiii. 19, 20).   *There they buried Abraham and Sarah his wife; there they buried Isaac and Rebekah his wife* (xlix. 31). There Jacob *buried Leah*, and thither was his own body brought to be buried, after its embalming far away in the land of the Pharaohs.

The mystery which to this day surrounds the cave is, says Dean Stanley, "a living witness of the unbroken local veneration with which the three religions of Jew, Christian, and Mussulman have honoured the great patriarch"—him of whom the Arabs still reverently speak as "The Friend of God."

<hr/>

hide; but after the agreement was concluded he cut the hide into thongs, and surrounded the whole of the space now forming the Haram."—*Dict. of Bible*, ii. 183.

Coined money is not mentioned in the Bible before the Babylonian captivity.   The Jews do not seem to have had coins of their own till about 140 B.C. (1 Maccabees xv. 6).   See British Museum specimen.

CHAPTER II

"I shall enlarge further on what concerns Egypt, because it
contains more wonders than any other country ; and because
there is none that contains so many works which are admirable
beyond expression."—HERODOTUS, ii. 35.

FOLLOWING the brilliant period marked by the XIIth
dynasty, there comes another gap in the history of
Egypt. From the XIVth to the XVIIIth dynasty
there are few monuments or buildings ; and the
records of foreign conquest give place to a silence
and a void, whose very limits we have, as yet, no
means of ascertaining.

It was probably at the beginning of the XIVth
dynasty that Egypt was overwhelmed by the
mysterious Asiatic invaders called Hyksos, or
"Shepherd kings."

"There came up from the East," says Manetho,
"in a strange manner, men of an ignoble race,
who had the confidence to invade our country,

and easily subdued it without a battle. And
when they had our rulers in their hands, they
burnt our cities, and demolished the temples of
the gods, and inflicted every kind of barbarity
upon the inhabitants, slaying some, and reducing
the wives and children of others to a state of
slavery. At length they made one of themselves
king, whose name was Salatis: he lived at Memphis, and rendered both the upper and lower
regions of Egypt tributary, and stationed garrisons
in places which were best adapted for that purpose." He rebuilt the strong city Avaris, "and
strongly fortified it with walls, and garrisoned it
with a force of two hundred and fifty thousand men
completely armed. To this city Salatis repaired in
summer-time, to collect his tribute, and pay his
troops, and to exercise his soldiers in order to
strike terror into foreigners." "All this nation was
styled Hycsos, that is the Shepherd kings; for
the first syllable, Hyc, in the sacred dialect
denotes a king, and Sos signifies a Shepherd;
but this only according to the vulgar tongue;
and of these is compounded the term Hycsos:
some say they were Arabians. This people who
were thus denominated Shepherd kings, and their

descendants, retained possession of Egypt during the period of five hundred and eleven years." [1]

Their rule seems, in fact, to have been a military occupation. The Hyksos left behind them no records, no public works, few monuments, little else but the memory of an "ignoble race."— "lepers" they are styled in the First Sallier Papyrus—who held Egypt in degrading subjection for an uncertain term of years, and were finally expelled after a "long and mighty war." [2] Their exact nationality is still a matter of uncertainty

---

[1] See Cory's *Fragments*, 169 (from Georgius Sycellus, Jos. *Cont. App.* etc.). Manetho wrote in Greek about 263 B.C. He was "high-priest and scribe" at Heliopolis, and lays before "the great and august King Ptolemy Philadelphus what I have gathered from the sacred books written by Hermes Trismegistus, our forefather." His work has been preserved to us only in fragments (quoted by other ancient writers), which often differ from the accounts given by Herodotus and Diodorus, but have been generally confirmed by the monumental inscriptions. We may add that it was also during the reign and at the instance of Ptolemy Philadelphus that the Greek translation of the Bible, called the Septuagint, was made by seventy elders. This, and not the original Hebrew, was the Bible used by our Lord and by the Apostles and Evangelists.

[2] "The duration of their dominion, which is variously estimated at 260, 511, and 900 years, is wholly uncertain, and will probably never be determined."—Rawlinson, *Herodotus*, ii. 397. 511 is the duration according to Manetho, as reported by Josephus.

and dispute. The few monuments of their time that have been discovered show a type of face with thick lips, high cheek-bones, and bushy beards—a type whose expression of stern vigour strongly contrasts with the "kindly urbanity" depicted upon the early Egyptian monuments. It is probable that the Hyksos hordes contained the offscourings of many nations ; but all we know with certainty is that with them came great bands of Hittites and Semites from Canaan— "foreign Phoenician kings" Manetho calls them, —who established in Egypt the worship of a supreme deity adapted from the Babylonian Sun-god Samas.

"The King Ra Apepi," says the First Sallier Papyrus, "chose the god Sutech as his lord, and was not the follower of any other god in the whole country." Now this Sutech was the great Hittite deity, who (borrowed like the Semitic Baal from the sun-worship of Babylonia) stood in the same relation to his Hittite worshippers as that in which Baal stood to the populations of Canaan ; and who, as the war-god of the foreigner, became to the native Egyptians Set or Typhon, the personification of evil, the brother and lifelong adversary of

Osiris. Thus in Josephus, Manetho says of Avaris, the Hyksos stronghold, "Now this city, according to the ancient theology, is a Typhonian city."

It is suggested that some of the Hittites who formed part of the Hyksos host, entering Egypt, settled down in the Delta, about the border city Zoan; while others remained in Southern Palestine. "*Thy mother was an Hittite,*" says Ezekiel to Jerusalem (xvi. 3, 45). Renan is further of opinion that it was in this "pays mixte" of the Delta that the "Phoenician" system of writing came into being, called forth by the necessity of trade intercourse between the various races, who to their own needs adapted the existing Egyptian hieroglyphics.[1] The two Hittite capitals, Hebron and Zoan or Tanis, whose name means "place of departure," evidently kept up relations one with another; and long years afterwards the Israelite city was proud to record the fact that it *was built seven years before Zoan in Egypt* (Numb. xiii. 22).

Naturally, therefore, *it pleased Pharaoh well, and his servants* (Gen. xlv. 16), when another Asiatic tribe came to settle in Egypt, perhaps to

[1] Renan, *Hist. du Peup.* i. 135. Sayce, *Fresh Light*, 86; *Hittites*, 132.

strengthen his hands against his native Egyptian subjects, and he readily welcomed Jacob and his sons when they migrated from Canaan. Joseph had only to *go up and shew Pharaoh and say unto him, " My brethren, and my father's house, which were in the land of Canaan, are come unto me ; and the men are shepherds, for their trade hath been to feed cattle ; and they have brought their flocks, and their herds, and all that they have "* (xlvi. 31, 32); the brethren had only to say, *" Thy servants are shepherds, both we, and also our fathers,"* and the welcome of the Pharaoh was assured. *" The land of Egypt is before thee,"* he said to Joseph ; *" in the best of the land make thy father and brethren to dwell ; in the land of Goshen let them dwell "* (xlvii. 6).

Every shepherd was *an abomination* to the native Egyptians, upon whose monuments they are always represented as a dirty and degraded race ; and in whom a fastidious cleanliness, as well as an intense dislike of foreigners (increased, if not originated, by their hatred of the Hyksos rule), were strongly marked features.[1]

---

[1] Herodotus notes that in his day " the swineherds, notwithstanding that they are of pure Egyptian blood, are forbidden

But under the Shepherd kings the Israelites were allowed to take possession of the land of Goshen, that pleasant tract, where, says the Greek historian, Mycerinus, when his doom was fixed, "had lamps prepared, which he lighted every day at eventime, and feasted and enjoyed himself unceasingly both day and night, moving about in the marsh country and the woods." And Joseph was made Keeper of the Granaries—a high official often represented upon the monuments with his signet ring and gold chain of office, and his reed and scroll wherewith to record his lord's possessions.

It is supposed that the mighty monarch who was able to say to Joseph, "*I am Pharaoh, and without thee shall no man lift up his hand or foot in all the land of Egypt*" (Gen. xli. 44), was Ra Apepi II., the last of the Hyksos kings, the worshipper of Set.[1]

to enter into any of the temples, which are open to all other Egyptians."—ii. 47. See also ii. 41.

"The hatred borne against shepherds by the Egyptians was not owing solely to their contempt for that occupation; this feeling originated in another and a far more powerful cause,— the previous occupation of their country by a pastor race, who had committed great cruelties during their possession of the country."—Wilkinson, *Ancient Egyptians*, ii. 16.

[1] The story of Joseph and Potiphar's wife finds a curious

But there has lately been discovered, at Bubastis, part of a seated Hyksos statue, upon which the royal name reads "Ian-Ra" or "Ra-Ian"; and it is said that when this was shown to a learned Mohammedan official in the museum then at Boulak, he exclaimed at once, "You have found the Pharaoh of Joseph. All our Arab books call him Reiyan." If so, it was for Ra-Ian (whom M. Naville distinguishes from Apepi, and identifies with Ianias, the fifth of Manetho's six Shepherd kings) that Joseph caused to be stored up, during the plenteous years, *corn as the sand of the sea, very much* (Gen. xli. 49); and for him that, when later *the famine was very sore*, he *bought all the land of Egypt . . . for the Egyptians sold every man his field, because the famine prevailed over them : so the land became Pharaoh's.* Then, and for all time since, have the fellaheen of Egypt been condemned to work for some foreign

counterpart in the hieratic Papyrus called "The Tale of the Two Brothers," once in the possession of Seti II. of the xixth dynasty, now in the British Museum.

The expression in Gen. xli. 40, "*according to thy word shall all my people be ruled*," is in the Hebrew "shall all my people *kiss*," alluding evidently to the usual eastern mode of signifying obedience by kissing the Firmán of the sovereign. See Wilkinson, *Ancient Egyptians*, ii. 24.

over-lord, counted fortunate if they kept for themselves the hundredth part of the fruit of their toil—

> *" So that they go about naked without clothing,*
> *And being an-hungred they carry the sheaves ;*
> *They make oil within the walls of these men ;*
> *They tread their winepresses, and suffer thirst."*
>
> Job xxiv. 10, R.V.

The Egyptians, says Josephus, "appear to have never, in all the past ages, had one day of freedom, no, not so much as from their own lords."

The change thus brought about in the ownership of the land is the greatest difference to be noted in the social life of Egypt, as shown on the monuments before and after the Hyksos rule. The monuments of the Old and Middle empires, the first or Pyramid series, of the ivth dynasty, and the xiith dynasty Tombs of Benihassan, show a state of civilisation varying hardly at all with the lapse of centuries. But in the monuments, on which every detail in the daily life of the great Ramesside kings of the New empire is depicted, we see that the land has entirely passed away from the people.[1]

---

[1] The exemption concerning the priest's land, *which became not Pharaoh's, for the priests had a portion assigned them of Pharaoh* (Gen. xlvii.), does not appear from the monuments

E

During all the time that the Shepherds ruled in the Delta, Egyptian dynasties seem to have borne a more or less independent sway at Thebes in Upper Egypt; and in the reign of Apepi II., when the "Lepers" were in Heliopolis, and the Egyptian Rasekenen, or Ta-āken, was "ruler in the southern region," the Hyksos king, growing jealous of his tributary's power, sent him an insulting order to provide men and materials for building a great temple to the stranger god Sutech. This order the worshipper of Ra received at first "silent, in great dismay" (*Rec.* viii. 4). Finally, goaded to revolt, he sent an army against the Shepherd king, "and a long and mighty war was carried on between them, till the Shepherds were overcome."[1] They were driven back into their stronghold of Avaris, where they made their last stand, and in the attack on which Ta-āken lost his life. Quite lately (1881) his mummy has been found in a hiding-place near the Valley of the Tombs of the Kings, at Thebes; and when it was unwrapped from the linen swathes,

but Herodotus mentions the privileges of the warriors and of the priestly caste, with regard to land (ii. 169). Cf. Diod. Sic. i. 73.

[1] Manetho. Cory, *Fragments*, 171.

which had evidently been put on in haste by unpractised hands, there was revealed the fact that Ta-āken had diéd a violent death upon the field of battle.

"The head was thrown back and lying low to the left. A large wound running across the right temple, a little above the frontal ridge, was partly concealed by long and scanty locks of hair. The lips were wide open and contracted into a circle, from which the front teeth, gums, and tongue protruded, the latter being held between the teeth and partly bitten through. The features, forcibly distorted, wore a very evident expression of acute suffering. . . . We already know that Ta-āken fought against the Shepherds . . . but till now we did not know that he died on the field. The Egyptians were evidently victorious in the struggle which took place over the corpse of their leader, or they would not have succeeded in rescuing it and in carrying it off the field. Being then and there hastily embalmed, it was conveyed to Thebes, where it received the rites of sepulture. These facts explain, not only the startling aspect of the mummy, but the irregular fashion of its embalmment."[1]

[1] M. Maspéro's Official Report, *Times*, 23rd July 1886.

The First Sallier Papyrus (*Rec.* viii. 1) throws great light upon the history of the early kings of the xviiith dynasty; so also do the inscriptions upon a tomb at Eileithyia belonging to an officer named Aahmes, who describes how, when he was yet "too young to have a wife," he served under Aahmes I., son of Ta-āken, in the war against the Hyksos kings. "We laid siege to the city of Avaris, and I had to fight on foot in the presence of his majesty. I was promoted to the ship called Cha-em-Mennefer (crowned in Memphis). . . . I obtained prizes; I carried off a hand, mention of which was made to the Reporter Royal, and there was given me the golden collar of valour. . . . We took Avaris. . . . His majesty slaughtered the Asiatic barbarians." Aahmes goes on to describe how he was at the head of the Egyptian soldiers in Naharaina (Mesopotamia) under Thothmes I., and was raised by him " to the dignity of Captain-general of the Marines." During his long term of office, he says, he "never left the king out of sight, from the king of Upper and Lower Egypt, the Ra-aa-peh-ti (Aahmes I.), the justified, to the king of Upper and Lower Egypt, the Ra-aa-Kheperu (Thothmes I.), the justified." He died and was buried in the reign of "Thothmes III., the ever-living." [1]

Aahmes I. (Amosis) was the successor of Ta-āken, who, finishing the work which his father had begun, finally drove out the Shepherd kings.

He founded the XVIIIth dynasty, under whom came the most brilliant period of Egyptian history, —a period during which most of the monuments now standing in Egypt were erected ; when Egypt "placed her frontiers where she would"; and when Thebes was the centre of a despotism which oppressed the whole world around.

The first, and one of the most remarkable, of these great XVIIIth dynasty conquerors was Thothmes I., grandson of Aahmes. He raised many obelisks and buildings in his native country, and was the earliest of the Egyptians who passed through the "land of Canaan " (as we find it called upon the monuments), defeating the numerous kings en-throned in its strong places, and penetrating into the far-off land of Mesopotamia, or Naharaina, where the great Chaldean monarchy of the days of Abraham had long since given place to a number

[1] *Rec.* vi. 7, 10 ; iv. 8.

of petty kingdoms, whose strongholds were Babel, Nineveh, and Assur.

Naharaina is described on the Assyrian monuments as being "in front of the land of the Hittites"; and it was Thothmes I. who, in the course of his conquests, resolving to "wash his heart" in the blood of that powerful people, began the long war which ended only in the reign of Rameses II.

On an xviiith dynasty tomb of a Theban prince named Rekh-ma-ra—"the oldest attempt to construct what we may call an ethnographic chart"— are found the earliest known representations of the Hittite race. They are so repulsively ugly that we should suspect the Egyptian artist of having caricatured his country's enemies, were it not that the faces exactly resemble the Hittite portraits upon their own bas-reliefs, and thus form a "convincing proof of the faithfulness of the Egyptian representations, as well as of the identity of the Hittites of the Egyptian inscriptions with the Hittites of Carchemish and Kappadokia."[1]

Thothmes II. was short-lived, and after his

[1] Sayce, *Hittites*, 101; *Races of the Old Testament*, 20, 39, 104, 132.

death, his consort and sister [1] Hatasou (sometimes called Hatshepsu, or Hasheps) continued to reign conjointly with their younger brother Thothmes III., until her death or dethronement. The monuments are silent as to her fate, and dark suggestions are thrown out in Egyptian histories as to her relations with her brothers, the first and second Thothmes. All that seems certain is that she was recognised as queen by her father, who calls her "Queen of the South and of the North," [2] and her position is thus a

---

[1] Isis, for whose "sake it is a custom among the Egyptians that they honour a queen" (D. i. 2), was the royal consort and sister of Osiris, who with him governed Amenti, the region of the dead. "This fabulous notion was supposed to have been the origin of a custom prevalent in Egypt from the earliest to the latest periods, which permitted brothers and sisters to marry; such an alliance being considered fortunate, in consequence of the example set by Isis and Osiris."—Wilkinson, *Ancient Egyptians*, iv. 385.

[2] "The Sun-god's path from east to west was supposed to divide space into two worlds—that of the south and that of the north. The king of Egypt, as son and heir of the Sun-god, claimed to be ruler of the two worlds—that is, of the entire universe."—*Rec.* xii. 128 n.

Maspéro, *Eg. Arch.* 288 n., describes the state chair of Hatshepsu exhibited in Manchester Jubilee Exhibition. "It is made of dark wood, apparently rosewood, the legs being shaped like bulls' legs, having silver hoofs, and a solid gold cobra snake twining round each leg. The arm-pieces are of

most interesting illustration of the status of women at that time in Egypt.

Hatasou, "the queen, the pure gold of monarchs," as she calls herself in her inscriptions, caused a great fleet to be built, which, braving the dangers of the "Very green," [1] sailed to Pount, or Arabia Felix, the Holy Land of the ancients.

Its "glad arrival in the West," bringing in-

ARABIAN QUEEN, CAPTIVE OF
HATASOU.

cense and ebony, ivory and gold and silver, leopard skins from the south, and apes and monkeys, is celebrated in brightly coloured bas - reliefs on Hatasou's great temple at Thebes— bas-reliefs which contain the earliest known repre- sentations of sea - going vessels. "Never has a convoy been made like this one, by any king since the

light wood, with cobra snakes carved upon the flat in low relief, each snake covered with hundreds of small silver annulets to represent the markings of the reptile."

[1] So the Egyptians called the sea. Maspéro, *Ancient Egypt and Assyria*, 160.

creation of the world," says the inscription (*Rec.* x. 14).

It is curious to think that the deformed little queen whom Hatasou's fleet brought back in triumph to Egypt, was a predecessor of that Queen of Sheba who, so many centuries later, "*came to Jerusalem with a very great train, with camels that bare spices*" (1 Kings x. 2). For Sheba, the modern Yemen in Arabia, was Pount, the land of incense, the Regio Cinnamonifera, of which Diodorus[1] says that it "breathes out all sorts of fragrant smells from the trees," so as to entertain "them that sail along by the coast at a great distance with its pleasures and delights "—

> " Sabean odours, from the spicy shore
> Of Arabie the blest."—MILTON.

The most remarkable of Hatasou's monuments seems to have been the great obelisk at Karnak, the tallest in the world; but when, after her fall, her brother Thothmes III. came to his full power, he caused her name to be erased from her monuments, and his own carved instead. In some the work was not carried out, says Wilkinson,[2]

---

[1] Diodorus, ii. 4, iii. 3. Maspéro, in *Eg. Arch.* 106, says Pount was on the African coast, south of Abyssinia.

[2] Sir G. Wilkinson in Rawlinson's *Herodotus*, ii. 355.

" with the care required to conceal the alterations,
and sentences of this kind frequently occur: 'King
Thothmes, *she* has made this work for *her* father
Amen';" but many of the monuments ascribed
to Thothmes were probably Hatasou's.

He succeeded, moreover, in having her name
omitted from the list of Egyptian kings; and
thus the reign of fifty-three years with which
the inscriptions credit Thothmes III., and the
date of which (1503-1449) has been accurately
determined by astronomical observations, almost
certainly includes the period of Hatasou's joint
sovereignty.

In any case, however, Egypt may be said to
have reached the zenith of her splendour under
his rule, and his reign is one of the most remarkable in the history of the Pharaohs. He is,
indeed, "the Alexander of Egyptian history," his
power extending from Ethiopia far into Asia. His
cartouches (the royal name with its surround-
ing oval) have been found in Assyria, and he is
even said to have kept a fleet upon the Euphrates.
His were the great obelisks which now stand in
London. and Rome, in Constantinople and New
York; and his cartouche, with its Disk and Sacred

Beetle,[1] may be seen on the sides of our own—
the so-called " Cleopatra's Needle " on the Thames
embankment. He left more monuments than any
Pharaoh, except the second Rameses, and there
are said to be "more bricks bearing his name
than that of any other king."

His triumphs were recorded upon the walls of
the granite sanctuary, which he added to the great
temple at Karnak, where he is represented as
doing homage to sixty-one of his predecessors ;
and long ages after his day the priests showed
these inscriptions to the Roman Germanicus.
" Legebantur," says Tacitus, " et indicta gentibus
tributa, pondus argenti et auri, numerus armorum
equorumque, et dona templis, ebur atque odores,
quasque copias frumenti et omnium utensilium
quæque natio penderet." [2]

" There is not any rebel to thee in the circle of
heaven," says one of his tablets; " they come
bearing their tribute on their backs, beseeching

---

[1] The divine name, or prenomen, of Thothmes III. was
Ra-men-Kheper—Ra the Sun-god, whose emblem was Aten the
Disk ; Men, or Amen, the god of Thebes ; and Kheper the
Scarabæus or Sacred Beetle, symbol of the future life.—King,
Cleopatra's Needle, 74.

[2] Mariette, *Monuments of Upper Egypt*, 177.

thy majesty"—"wretched Kush" and "miserable princes of Naharaina," bringing ebony and ivory and panther skins, precious metals and porcelain, slaves and cattle and spices. This is no vain boast—"Heaven knows it, earth knows it, the whole world sees it hourly," says the king (*Rec.* ii. 32-57).

It is upon one of the tombs of his period that the curious process of brickmaking is represented, which tallies so exactly with that described in Exodus; showing, as it does, the hardness of the work, the tales of bricks, the bringing of the straw, and the Egyptian taskmasters set over the foreign workmen, these being easily distinguished from the natives by the colour in which they are drawn. The captives are said to "perform their service with a mind full of love for the king," but there is the significant addition that "the overseer speaks thus to the labourers at the building, ' *The stick is in my hand; be not idle.*'"

With a thrill of interest we read of the finding of this great king among the royal remains near the Valley of Tombs. Within the wooden mummy-case were wreaths of flowers, larkspurs, acacias, and lotuses, looking, it is said, as if they

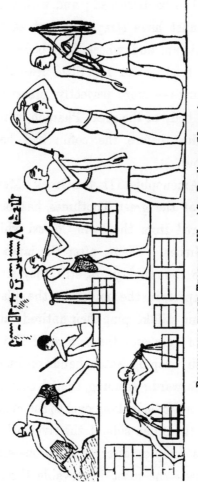

BRICKMAKING UNDER THOTHMES III.—After Rawlinson (Murray).

had been lately dried in the sun, so plainly were their colours still to be discerned; and with them a wasp, which must have strayed in just as the coffin was closed up, and whose frail body had thus been preserved entire for little less than thirty-five centuries — more perfectly preserved, indeed, than the body of the great Pharaoh, which crumbled into dust before the coffin had been opened for an hour.

Amenhotep (Amenophis) III., the Greek "Memnon," grandson of the great Thothmes, has been chiefly remembered from the Twin Colossi which he reared at Thebes. There, after the lapse of more than three thousand years, still they sit— "together, yet apart, in the midst of the plain, serene and vigilant, still keeping their untired watch over the lapse of ages and the eclipse of Egypt. ... There they sit, keeping watch, hands on knees, gazing straight forward; seeming, though so much of the faces is gone, to be looking over to the monumental piles on the other side of the river, which became gorgeous temples, after these throne-seats were placed here—the most immovable thrones that have ever been established on this earth." [1]

---

[1] Martineau, *Eastern Life*, i. 84, 289.

Besides being a magnificent constructor of palaces and temples, Amenhotep III. was a mighty conqueror, and he counted the captives whom he brought back to Egypt to be his slaves, like cattle, by the " head."

During all his reign he seems to have been associated, in peace and in war, with the kings of Canaan and of Naharaina, or Mitanni; and his archives are full of letters and despatches from the East. Amongst others there are several from the priest-king of Salem, Ebed-Tob, who, though a vassal and a tributary of the Pharaoh, insists that he holds his royal dignity not from Egypt, but in virtue of his priesthood, by an oracle from the " mighty King," the God of Peace—just as Melchizedek was *King of Salem, Priest of the most High God.*[1]

Amenhotep took to wife Tii, daughter of the Mesopotamian king, and on a scarabaeus, now in the British Museum, is an inscription celebrating his marriage with "the great royal lady Tii the living," "the marvel, the daughter of the chief of Naharaina" (*Rec.* xii. 39)—a marriage which had strange consequences for the land of Egypt.

[1] Sayce, *Expository Times*, December 1891.

" If," says a writer in the *Century*, speaking of
Tii's portrait among the Tombs of the Queens—
" If Rebekah and Rachel were only half so fair
as she, they were well worth a journey away to
Mesopotamia to win."   And it is suggested that
perhaps they were not unlike in another very
different respect.   For when Rachel, on the eve
of the furtive departure from Mesopotamia, *stole
away the images that were her father's* (Gen. xxxi.
19), she must have done so because she trusted in
them as gods.   Tii, too, trusted in the gods of her
fathers, and carried with her to Egypt the Babylonian Sun-god Samas.   We may thus fancy her as
causing all those religious troubles which distracted
Egypt at the close of the xviiith dynasty.

For her son, Amenhotep IV., was a devoted worshipper of the new divinity.   He changed his name
from Amenhotep to Khuen-Aten (Glory or Splendour of the Solar Disk) ; and, perhaps to escape
the opposition of the priests, moved his capital
away from the ancient temples of Thebes, farther
north, to the spot now marked by the mounds of
Tel-el-Amarna, where he built a new capital and
gave himself up altogether to the new worship.
Half Asiatic in descent, wholly Asiatic in faith,

he surrounded himself with Semitic and Hittite officers and courtiers. He and the kings who came after him, and who occupy little more than a generation, either figure in the lists as "Strangers," or their names are omitted altogether; and thus we see that the rise of the XIxth dynasty—of the kings *which knew not Joseph* (Ex. i. 8)—did, in very truth, mark a reaction against Semitic influence and power.[1]

KHUEN-ATEN ADORING THE SUN'S DISK.

Rameses I., the earliest of these XIxth dynasty kings, was succeeded, after a short and uneventful reign, by his more famous son, Seti I., who sought to legitimatise his rule by marrying the daughter of Amenhotep and of the Mesopotamian Tii. Herein we may see the explanation

---

[1] *Rec.* N. S. ii. 60 ; *Races of the Old Testament,* 98.

of that mysterious passage in Isaiah, in which it is
said that God's people *went down aforetime into
Egypt to sojourn there ; and the Assyrian oppressed
them without cause* (lii. 4).   But all this belongs
rather to the region of fancy than of fact.   Seti's
real claim to dominion no doubt lay in his own
vigorous personality ; and a genealogical table of
thirty centuries gone by will not be read by the
learned without a smile.

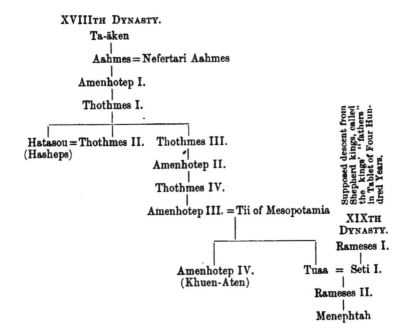

XVIIITH DYNASTY.
  Ta-āken
  Aahmes = Nefertari Aahmes
  Amenhotep I.
  Thothmes I.

Hatasou = Thothmes II.   Thothmes III.
(Hasheps)
                        Amenhotep II.
                        Thothmes IV.
                  Amenhotep III. = Tii of Mesopotamia

                Amenhotep IV.   Tuaa = Seti I.
                (Khuen-Aten)
                                  Rameses II.
                                  Menephtah

Supposed descent from Shepherd kings, called the kings' "fathers" in Tablet of Four Hundred Years.

XIXTH DYNASTY.
Rameses I.

Like the conquering kings of the xiith and xviiith dynasties, Seti I. carried his arms far and wide. He prosecuted with vigour the great war begun by Thothmes I. against the Hittites, who had taken advantage of the internal troubles in Egypt to push southwards, and to garrison many of the Syrian cities formerly held by the Pharaohs. The archives of Tel-el-Amarna contain many a cuneiform clay tablet, despatched by the Egyptian governors in Syria, praying their royal masters to send more troops to be used against the invader. From this time forward, indeed, it becomes possible to speak of a Hittite Empire—the newcomer had, as it were, driven a wedge between the Semites of the West and of the East; and the tongue of Babylonia gradually ceased to be the language of official intercourse.

But with Seti I. the power of Egypt had revived, and the Hittites were driven back from many of the strongholds they had captured in Syria. "Pharaoh is a jackal which rushes leaping through the Hittite land," says the song of triumph; "he is a grim lion exploring the hidden ways of all regions; he is a powerful bull with a pair of sharpened horns. He has struck down the Asiatics ; he has thrown to the ground the Khita; he has slain their princes ; he has overwhelmed them in their own blood; he has passed among them as a flame of fire ; he has brought them to nought." "They lay on the ground in their blood, so that none could escape his fury to tell his prowess to their people."

Seti also attacked the Cushites or Ethiopians, and returned to his capital victorious on every hand,—"on the south to the arms of the winds, and on the north to the Great Sea."

On the walls of the beautiful pillared hall which he built at Karnak—"even in its ruins one of the grandest sights that the world contains" [1] —appears many an inscription, vainglorious, as are all the inscriptions of these monarchs of the ancient world, in which Seti I. records his victory and his personal valour.

In the list of his prisoners are mentioned the Javans Iones (supposed to be the Greeks), the

[1] "No language can convey an idea of its beauty, and no artist has yet been able to reproduce its form so as to convey to those who have not seen it an idea of its grandeur. . . . The beauty and massiveness of the forms, and the brilliancy of their coloured decorations, all combine to stamp this as the greatest of man's architectural works."— Fergusson, *Hist. of Architecture*, i. 119, 120.

Eastern Shepherds, the Khita or Hittites, the men of Naharaina or Mesopotamia, the Ruten-nu, the Punt Somali of South Arabia, the Shasu or Bedouin tribes, and many towns of Central Asia, besides tribes of Nubia and Abyssinia, and the Aperu, supposed by many to be the children of Israel.

"In the countries where the natives withstood his attack, and fought gallantly for their liberties," says the Greek historian of his Sesostris, "he erected pillars, on which he inscribed his own name and country, and how that he had here reduced the inhabitants to subjection by the might of his arms: when, on the contrary, they submitted readily and without a struggle, he inscribed on the pillars, in addition to these particulars, an emblem to mark that they were a nation of women—that is, unwarlike and effeminate " (H. ii. 102).

Very early Seti associated his son Rameses with himself in the sovereignty; and the two together, with their long reigns, their power and glory, their buildings and their conquests, have eclipsed the fame of old Usertesen, and taken his place as the Sesostris of Greek literature.

But it is as the Pharaohs of the Israelitish oppression that father and son are chiefly interesting to us. Almost certainly Seti I. was *the new king who knew not Joseph* (Ex. i. 8), and who so ruthlessly determined to put an end to that foreign domination under which a Hebrew had been made *ruler over all the land of Egypt* (Gen. xli. 43). Almost certainly he was the Pharaoh who *said unto his people, Behold, the people of the children of Israel are more and mightier than we: Come on, let us deal wisely with them; lest they multiply, and it come to pass, that, when there falleth out any war, they join also unto our enemies, and fight against us, and so get them up out of the land* (Ex. i. 9). Almost certainly Seti was the ruler who made the lives of the Hebrew people *bitter with hard bondage, in mortar, and in brick, and in all manner of service in the field* (i. 14). Almost certainly he was the Pharaoh who issued that ruthless order, *Every son that is born ye shall cast into the river* (i. 22). Almost certainly he was the father of the kindly princess who *had compassion on* the babe in the ark among *the flags by the river's brink,* and *called his name Moses,* saying, *Because I drew him out of the water.*[1]

---

[1] Hebrew, *Màshàh*, "to draw out." Josephus derives the name from the Coptic words *mo, water,* and "*uses,* such as are

The mummy of Seti I. has been recovered, and it now lies in the museum of the Ghizeh Palace for all to see, a proof that "the sculptors of Thebes and Abydos did not flatter the Pharaoh when they gave him that delicate, sweet, and smiling profile, which is the admiration of travellers."[1]

Rameses II. was, as we have seen, very early associated with his father in the government, possibly because Seti wished to secure the full advantage of his son's descent from the royal house of the xviiith dynasty.

"In thy childhood what thou saidst took place for the welfare of the land," says an inscription.[2] "When thou wert a boy, with the youth's locks of hair, no monument saw the light without thy command; no business was done without thy knowledge. Thou wert raised to be a governor of the land when thou wert a youth, and countedst 10 full years."

saved out of it" (ii. 10, 6); but in all probability the name Moses is derived from the Egyptian *Mes* or *Mesu*, "son," to commemorate the fact that he was the adopted son of the Pharaoh's daughter. We find the same word in the name of Rameses, "Ra-mesu," son of Ra, the hawk-headed Sun-god.

[1] Maspéro, *Times*, 23rd July 1886.

[2] Robinson, *Pharaohs of Bondage and Exodus*, 58. See *Records*, viii. 77, 78.

And Rameses says of himself in an inscription
at Abydos : "My father presented me publicly to

SETI AND RAMESES.[1]

the people ; I was a boy on his lap, and he spake
thus : I will have him crowned as king, for I

[1] Notice the side-plait of hair worn by Egyptian youths, and
laid aside either when they attained manhood, or possibly, in
the case of a prince, only on accession to the throne. Note

desire to behold his grandeur, while I am still
alive. Then came forward the courtiers to place
the double crown upon my head. And my father
said : Place the regal circlet on his brow."

" We often hear it said that Egypt was governed
by a theocracy," says Stanley; "that is, as the word
is meant when so applied, by a priestly caste.
This is not the answer given by her own authentic
monuments. Who is the colossal figure that sits,
repeated again and again, at the entrance of every
temple ? Who is it that rides in his chariot, leading diminutive nations captive behind him ? To
whom is it, in the frontispiece of every gateway,
that the gods give the falchion of destruction,
with the command to 'slay, and slay, and slay ' ?
Whose sculptured image do we see in the interior

also the royal Uraeus serpent worn on the forehead by every
Egyptian king. It was supposed to think and fight for him,
to guide him by its counsels, and to slay his enemies in battle
by its fiery breath.

The Egyptians, in their drawings, preferred profiles for faces,
full-face for bust, sideways for legs, and "did not hesitate to
combine these contradictory points of view in one single figure.
The head is almost always given in profile, but is provided with
a full-face eye and placed upon a full-face bust. The full-face
bust adorns a trunk seen from a three-quarters point of view,
and this trunk is supported upon legs depicted in profile."—
Maspéro, *Eg. Arch.* 171.

of the temple, brought into the most familiar relations with highest powers, equal in form and majesty, suckled by the greatest goddess, fondled by the greatest god, sitting beside them, arm entwined within arm, in the recesses of the most holy place ? It is no priest, or prophet, or magician, or saint, but the king only — the Pharaoh, the Child of the Sun, the beloved of Ammon. And if there is one king who towers above all the rest in all the long succession, it is he whose name first dimly appears to us in the history of the Exodus, the great Rameses, the Sesostris of the classical writers " (i. 77).

" If," says an inscription, "thou formest a plan at night, it is realised in the day; and again if thou hast said to the waters, Come out of the mountain, the celestial water comes, according to thy word." [1]

Besides his doubly royal descent, Rameses was, or wished to appear, descended from the ancient Shepherd kings ; for in the Tablet of Four Hundred Years, lately discovered at Tanis, we find him dating his era from the reign of the Hyksos king Set-Apepi, and doing honour to Sutech, the

[1] Birch, *Egypt*, 124.

Hittite deity, whom the Hyksos had adopted (see p. 44). "His majesty ordered that a great tablet of stone should be made, in the great name of his fathers," says the inscription; "for the sake of setting up the name of the father of his fathers" (*Rec.* iv. 36).

Judging from his type of face, it is thought possible that Hyksos blood may have flowed in his veins; but whether descended from the Hyksos kings or no, and whether his mother's Asiatic ancestry had or had not an appreciable effect upon the race, Rameses was certainly of a refined Asiatic type, very different from the coarse-featured kings of the earlier part of the xviiith dynasty.[1]

In his case, however, as in the case of his father Seti, prowess in the field and personal force of character probably counted for far more, in making and keeping his dominion, than any lineage or descent. His mummy, unwrapped from its countless folds of exquisitely fine orange and rose-coloured linen, lies now in the museum at Ghizeh; and it is no fancy that sees in that terrible face "an air of sovereign majesty, of

[1] Birch, *Egypt*, 129; Sayce, *Races of the O. T.* 98.

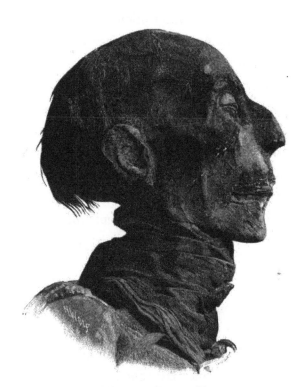

MUMMY OF RAMESES II.

resolve and of pride "[1]—an air of haughty disdain for human suffering and weakness.

The first and many later campaigns of Rameses II. were directed against the people of Cush or Ethiopia, but the great event of his reign was his campaign against the Khita in his fifth year. This is commemorated in the 3rd Sallier Papyrus,[2] containing the heroic poem of Pentaour, which has been called the Iliad of Egypt, and in which we read grandiloquent accounts of his Majesty's glory and personal prowess. It was during one of the battles in this campaign that Rameses, being cut off from all his army, and finding himself alone among the enemy, performed the prodigies of valour which form the theme of the poet, and which the king himself was never tired of recording upon his monuments—upon the Ramesseum at Thebes, and upon the walls of the great temples at Karnak, and at Abou-Simbel. "I had come upon 2500 pairs of horses," the poet makes him say; "I was in the midst of them; then were they overthrown before my

---

[1] Prof. Maspéro's Report, quoted Robinson's *Pharaohs*, 71.
[2] Now in British Museum. *Rec.* ii. 67-78 ; Brugsch, *Hist.* i. 140.

steeds. Not one of them raised his hand to fight; their heart shrank within them, their limbs gave way, they could not hurl the dart, nor had they strength to thrust with the spear. As crocodiles fall into the water, so I made them fall; they tumbled headlong over one another. I slew them; my pleasure was that not one of them should look behind him, nor any return. Each fell, and none raised himself up again."

"What to thy heart are those Asiatics?" he says to his charioteer Menna. "Amen brings very low them who know not God, he brightens not his face for millions of them." "My chariots and my archers have forsaken me," he cries aloud to Amen;[1] "not one remains with me to fight for me. Where art thou, Amen, my Father in heaven? Behold, can the father forget his child? Have

---

[1] The royal title of Rameses the Great is "Ra-user-ma Setep-en-ra Mer-amen Ra-mesu"—Sun, strong in truth, approved of the Sun, loved of Amen, son of the Sun (*Rec.* ii. 76).

Amen, chief god of Thebes, appears often in the inscriptions of this age as the supreme deity, the "One, Maker of Existences" (*Rec.* ii. 132). Ra, the Sun-god, and Tum or Atum, the setting Sun, are identified with him. The name is variously spelt Amon, Amen, Amun, by the different authors I have quoted: it has seemed to me best to adopt an uniform spelling throughout.

I ever trusted in my own strength? as I went and as I stood was not my countenance turned towards thee? Have I not ever done according to the words of thy mouth, and followed after thy mighty counsels? O thou great god of Egypt, destroy the people who surround me. . . . Out of my full heart have I called to thee, O my Father Amen! I am surrounded by the numberless people of all lands. Alone am I, no other is with me. My chariots and my archers have fled. . . . But Amen is better to me than myriads of archers, than millions of chariots, than ten thousand chosen youths. There is no help in the sons of men, for Amen stands higher than they."

At length, in the twenty-first year of Rameses, the long war with the Khita, which may, in the perspective of history, be said to have been begun by Thothmes I., was brought to an end; and a treaty of peace was concluded, which remains to this day, sculptured on the outer wall of the great temple at Karnak. The inscription shows how powerful were the now long-forgotten race who could thus treat on equal terms with one of the greatest monarchs the world has ever known; and this view is confirmed by the modern

discovery that the huge figure cut in the rock
of the Pass of Karabel, "between Sardis and
Smyrna," which Herodotus professed to have
seen, and ascribed to his Sesostris, was not the
Egyptian Pharaoh, "but a symbol of the far-
reaching power and influence of his mighty
opponents."[1]

"There came a royal herald," says the treaty;
"the grand duke of Khita, Khita-sira, had sent
to the king to beg for peace of King Ra-user-ma,
approved of the Sun, Son of the Sun, Ramessu-
Meriamen, endowed with life for ever and ever,
like his father the Sun continually . . . chief of
Rulers, whose boundaries extend to every land at
his pleasure. . . . Behold; Khita-sira the grand
duke of Khita covenants . . . with Ra-user-ma,
approved by the Sun, the great ruler of Egypt
from this day forth, that good peace and good
brotherhood shall be between us for ever. He shall
fraternise with me, he shall be at peace with
me, and I will fraternise with him, I will be
at peace with him for ever" (*Rec.* iv. 25). And
the treaty ends with some " extradition " clauses,
which form the earliest example of their kind,

[1] Sayce, *Hittites*, 65 ; see *Herodotus*, ii. 106.

and which prove how advanced in humanity was the law of nations at that time.

Later, the alliance was cemented by a marriage between the Pharaoh and Khita-Sira's daughter, who received the name of Ur-maat-Neferu-Ra. "The king's eldest daughter stands forward at the head of her people," says an inscription, "to soften the heart of King Rameses II.—a great inconceivable wonder. She herself knew not the impression which her beauty made." [1]

For the rest of his long reign—a reign of sixty-seven years, during fifty of which he was sole sovereign—Rameses, "the war-god of the world" (*Rec.* vi. 15), was free to devote himself to those mighty works of architecture and irrigation, upon which, rather than on his campaigns, his fame has rested. He finished the great canal begun by his father, which connected the Nile with the Red Sea ; he adorned Egypt from end to end with statues and obelisks ; he built the great temples at Abou-Simbel ; and at the towered gateway of his palace-temple at Thebes, the Ramesseum (called by the Greeks the tomb of Osymandyas), he erected that colossal statue of himself, in red granite

---

[1] Brugsch, *Egypt*, new ed., 294.

G

from Syene, which has been the wonder of all ages.[1]

"By some extraordinary catastrophe the statue has been thrown down, and the Arabs have scooped their mill-stones out of his face, but you can still see what he was—the largest statue in

---

[1] "Thebes spreads itself on both banks of the Nile, just as London and Paris extend over both banks of the Thames and Seine. On the right bank are the temples of Karnak and of Luxor." On the left bank, going from N. to S., are Seti I.'s temple of Goornah, Hatasou's temple of Deir-el-bahari (see p. 56), the Ramesseum, the Colossi of Amenhotep III. (see p. 62), and Rameses III.'s temple of Medinet-Abou. (Mariette's *Monuments of Upper Egypt*, 145 and *seq.*) The great temple of Karnak—which, says Mr. S. Poole, "is, from its stupendous size, among temples what the great Pyramid is among tombs" (*Cities*, 59)—is supposed to have been begun by Usertesen I., little of whose work, however, now remains. Thothmes I. added to it, and Hatasou erected the tall obelisks. Thothmes III. added the Hall of Ancestors, where he is represented as doing homage to sixty-one of his predecessors; while Seti I. began, and Rameses II. finished, the beautiful Hall of Columns (see p. 68). The Ramesseum was called by the Greeks the Tomb of Osymandyas, and, speaking of the great statue, Diodorus says: "Upon it is this inscription—I am Osymandias, King of kings; if any would know how great I am, and where I lie, let him excel me in any of my works" (D. i. 4). See the "Ozymandias" of Shelley. On the left bank of the river, too, on the western barrier of the Theban plain, are the tombs where lay *all the kings in glory, every one in his own house* (Is. xiv. 18).

the world. Far and wide that enormous head
must have been seen, eyes, mouth, and ears. Far
and wide you must have seen his vast hands
resting on his elephantine knees. . . . Nothing
which now exists in the world can give any
notion of what the effect must have been when
he was erect.   Nero towering above the Colosseum
may have been something like it, but he was of
bronze, and Rameses was of solid granite. Nero
was standing without any object; Rameses was
resting in awful majesty after the conquest of the
whole of the then known world. No one who
entered that building, whether it were temple or
palace, could have thought of anything else but
that stupendous being who thus had raised
himself up above the whole world of gods and
men." [1]

No wonder that in the great inscription at
Abou-Simbel the god Phtah is represented as
saying, "King Rameses, I grant thee to cut
the mountains into statues, immense, gigantic,
everlasting; I grant that foreign lands find for

[1] Stanley, *Sinai and Palestine*, xxxviii. A colossus which
must have been 313 tons heavier has, however, been discovered
by Mr. Flinders Petrie at Tanis (Edwards, *Pharaohs*, 53).

COLOSSUS AT ABOU-SIMBEL.

thee precious stone to inscribe the monuments with thy name" (*Rec.* xii. 89).

Finally, Rameses finished the great wall begun by his father, for the protection of Egypt against the Asiatics on her north-eastern frontier; and upon the line of this wall his toiling captives *built for Pharaoh treasure cities, Pithom and Raamses* [1] — "established on the earth like the four pillars of the sky," says the inscription.[2]

---

[1] Ex. i. 11. The construction of Rameses is mentioned in two Papyri now in the Leyden collection, in which a scribe named Kauitzir reports that he has "followed the instructions which my Lord gave me, namely, to give food to the soldiers as well as to the Asiatics who bring the stones to the great town of King Rameses-Meramen." There also exists a Papyrus letter, beginning, "The Clerk Panbesa salutes his Lord," which contains a poetic description of the town, the sentences, as is usual in Egyptian poems, having red dots placed above them to show the lines. "I found it flourishing in good things without a rival, like the foundations of Thebes, the abode of felicity. Its meadows are filled with all good things, it is well provisioned daily. Its pools are filled with fish, its ponds with fowl; its fields are verdant with grass. . . . Gladness dwells within it, none speaks scorn of it."—*Rec.* vi. 13.

[2] *Rec.* xii. 89. Pithom (the site of which has now been identified, twelve miles west of Ismailia, on the spot where in 1882 the English fought the battle of Kassassin) was Pa-Tum, the House or Abode of Tum, the setting sun. Besides this sacred or ecclesiastical name, it was called by the secular name

For Sesostris, says the Greek historian, made
use "of the multitudes whom he had brought
with him from the conquered countries, partly to
drag the huge masses of stone which were moved
in the course of his reign to the temple of
Vulcan (Ptah), partly to · dig the numerous
canals with which the whole of Egypt is inter-
sected " (H. ii. 108). And Diodorus adds
that he "made many fair and stately works,
admirable both for their cost and contrivance,
by which he both advanced his own immortal
praise, and procured unspeakable advantages to
the Egyptians, with perfect peace and security
for the time to come. For, beginning first with
what concerned the gods, he built a temple in all
the cities of Egypt, to that god whom every
particular place most adored ; and he employed
none of the Egyptians in his works, but finished
all by the labours of the captives ; and therefore
he caused an inscription to be made upon all the

of Sukut, and is thus the Succoth of the first stage of the
Exodus. It is also the Heroöpolis of the Septuagint. The
excavations show that, while the whole city is built of brick,
the upper courses are of an inferior quality, made without any
binding straw or reeds. The site of Raamses has not yet been
ascertained (Edwards, *Pharaohs*, 44-50).

temples thus—'None of the natives were put to labour here'" (i. 4).

Small wonder, then, that when, to use the significant phrase of Scripture, "*in process of time,*" the long reign which had extended over the better part of a century came to an end, the Pharaoh's death found the children of Israel sighing *by reason of their bondage* (Ex. ii. 23). For at least two generations their lives had been made *bitter with hard bondage, in mortar, and in brick, and in all manner of service in the field,* toiling in the black earth,[1] under the blazing sun of Egypt, with taskmasters set over them *to afflict them with their burdens* (Ex. i.).

Under Rameses II. Egyptian power and Egyptian art undoubtedly reached their highest point. It was the Augustan age of Egypt; the signs of her decay were hardly as yet to be discerned; and when we think of her grandeur and her glory, it is difficult to attach any importance to the Jewish tradition which says that the Pharaohs were filled with fear of their Hebrew captives. "And a royal

---

[1] Egypt is called Chemi, the black land, the land of Ham, on the monuments; and, according to Plutarch, this arises from the blackness of the soil (Rawlinson, *Herodotus,* ii. 23).

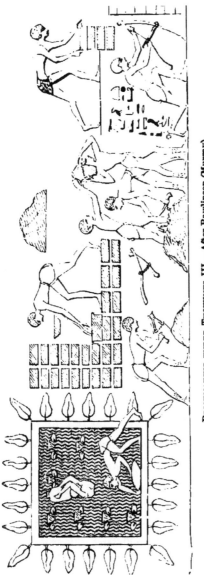

BRICKMAKING UNDER THOTHMES III.—After Rawlinson (Murray).

decree went forth over all the land of Egypt and Goshen, commanding all the inhabitants, both Egyptians and Hebrews, to build. Pharaoh himself set the example by taking trowel and basket in hand, and putting a brick mould on his neck. Whoever saw this hastened to do likewise, and all who were reluctant were stimulated by the overseers with these words, 'See how the king works. Will you not imitate his activity?' . . . By degrees the Egyptian workmen were withdrawn, yet the Hebrews were paid the regular wage. When a year and four months had elapsed, not an Egyptian was to be seen making bricks and building, and the wage was stopped for the future; but the Hebrews were kept to their work. If at evening the tale of bricks were not made up, then, in place of the deficient bricks, even though only one brick was short, they were to take the children of those who had not made up their task, and to build them into the wall in place of bricks." [1]

The legend is no doubt extravagant and absurd. But we must remember that the wall on the north-eastern frontier of Egypt, which Seti began and

[1] Baring Gould, *Old Testament Characters*, ii. 65-80.

which Rameses II. finished, was in itself a confession of weakness. No such bulwark had been
needed under Thothmes III., in the days when
Egypt "placed her frontiers where she would";
and when Seti and Rameses were succeeded by
the weak and cowardly Menephtah, then the
change in the fortunes of the country quickly
made itself felt.

"Durant le long règne de Ramsès II.," says M.
Renan, "toute idée de révolte fut impossible. Mais
les grandeurs militaires de ce règne et les con-
structions extraordinaires qui le signalèrent, pro-
duisirent leur effet ordinaire. Les dernières années
du Louis XIV. égyptien furent marquées par une
forte décadence. Le règne de Ménephtah, son suc-
cesseur, vit le commencement des revers" (i. 157).

The reign of Menephtah seems to have been
passed in constant and often unsuccessful conflict
with the forces which were undermining the greatness of his country.

In his fifth year Egypt was attacked by a
great confederation of five nations, including the
Achaeans, or Greeks ;[1] and though these were for

---

[1] "In this campaign the name of the Achaians first appears
applied to the Greeks, called before Hanebu, or Ionians, and

the time defeated in a great pitched battle which took place in the Delta, this was not owing to the personal prowess of the monarch himself. For before the day came on which he had promised to place himself at the head of his troops, he "saw in a dream," so he declared, "as it were a figure of the god Phtah, standing to prevent the advance of the king "—of Mer-en-Phtah, his beloved. The vision told him to "make a stand," letting his troops advance alone against the enemy, and this seasonable advice the monarch appears to have accepted with alacrity (*Rec.* iv. 3).

His monuments represent him to have been

---

does not recur. It has been recognised as the genuine name of the Greeks in the Homeric times, and to have been so for a period not longer than 140 years. . . . The Khita have been supposed also to be the *Ketaioi* of the Odyssey ; and the Exodus and the Trojan war to have occurred, if not exactly at the same time, yet closely after one another."—Birch, *Egypt*, 132.

It is to this movement of nations that M. Renan refers the establishment of the Philistines upon the coasts of Canaan, reminding us that at the Exodus God did not lead his people *through the way of the Philistines, though that was near; for God said, Lest peradventure the people repent when they see war, and they return to Egypt* (Ex. xiii. 17). Later, the Philistines became the masters of Israel, and, established on the coast, gave their name to the whole country, which became to the Greeks the "land of the Philistines"—Palestine (i. 157, 345 ; ii. 32).

neither a soldier nor an administrator, but "one whose mind was turned almost exclusively towards the chimeras of sorcery and magic"; and possibly he was the blind "Pheron, son of Sesostris," whose "impious violence" is chronicled by Herodotus (ii. 111).

He added very little to the great architectural works of his forefathers, but seems to have devoted some attention to the Delta, and to have beautified the small palace-temple at Tanis, where several obelisks bear his name, and which was evidently a favourite royal residence in the days when those "*marvellous things*" were done *in the field of Zoan* (Ps. lxxviii. 12), and when the Pharaoh, as we learn from the historian of the people whom he oppressed, *also called the wise men and the sorcerers*, bidding the magicians of Egypt do *also in like manner with their enchantments.*

But though Menephtah was not a great constructor, he was in all probability the tyrant who laid upon the Hebrew people the same tale of bricks as heretofore, even while commanding that they should no longer be provided with straw for binding the clay;[1] and who replied to their

---

[1] The ordinary Egyptian brick of to-day is a mere oblong

piteous pleading with the answer which has risen so readily to the lips of tyrants in all ages, " *Ye are idle, ye are idle* " (Ex. v. 17).

"It is impossible," says Stanley, "as we read the description of the Plagues, not to feel how much of force is added to it by a knowledge of the peculiar customs and character of the country in which they occurred. It is not an ordinary river that is turned into blood; it is the sacred, beneficent, solitary Nile, the very life of the state and of the people. . . . It is not an ordinary nation that is struck by the mass of putrefying vermin lying in heaps by the houses, the villages and the fields, or multiplying out of the dust of the desert sands on each side of the Nile valley. It is the cleanliest of all the ancient nations, clothed in white linen, anticipating in their fastidious delicacy and ceremonial purity the habits of modern and northern Europe. It is not the ordinary cattle that died in the field, or ordinary fish that died in the river, or ordinary reptiles

block of mud mixed with chopped straw and a little sand, and dried in the sun. Burnt bricks were hardly used at all before the Roman period. Brick was the material of the civil and military architecture of the Pharaohs ; the more durable stone that of their temples (Maspéro, *Eg. Arch.* 3, 4, 43).

that were overcome by the rod of Aaron. It is
the sacred goat of Mendes, the ram of Ammon, the
calf of Heliopolis, the bull Apis, the crocodile of
Ombos, the perch of Esneh. It is not an ordinary land of which the flax and the barley, and
every green thing in the trees, and every herb of
the field, are smitten by the two great calamities
of storm and locust. It is the garden of the
ancient eastern world — the long line of green
meadow and cornfield, and groves of palm and
sycamore and fig-tree, from the Cataracts to the
Delta, doubly refreshing from the desert which it
intersects, doubly marvellous from the river
whence it springs " (i. 100).

" Hail to thee, O Nile,"

says a hymn of the time of Menephtah,

" Thou shewest thyself in this land
    Coming in peace, giving life to Egypt . . .
    Overflowing the gardens created by Ra ;
    Giving life to all animals,
    Watering the land without ceasing :
    The way of heaven descending . . .
    He shineth, then the land exulteth !
    All things created receive nourishment . . .
    Bringer of food ! Great Lord of Provisions !
    Creator of all good things,
    Lord of Terrors and of choicest joys !"—*Rec.* iv. 107.

There is said to be evidence upon the monuments that Seti II.—the only son of Menephtah, *the first-born of Pharaoh, that sat on his throne* —died at an early age. There are said to be inscriptions which tell that he "governed Egypt in behalf of his father"[1]—inscriptions in which his name is followed by the death-sign Ma-Kheru, which means one "justified," he who is "proclaimed righteous" at the judgment-seat of Osiris. And the suggestion is that Seti Menephtah met his death on that awful night when *there was a great cry in Egypt; for there was not a house where there was not one dead* —on the night which witnessed the first Passover.

It has been suggested, too, that after the death of Menephtah's only son, Moses (as the adopted son of a princess[2] of the royal house) might have had

---

[1] *Century Magazine*, May 1887, Sept. 1889.

[2] According to Josephus her name was Thermuthis. Georgius (Syncellus) calls her "the daughter of Pharaoh, Thermuthis, who was also called Pharia." Other writers speak of her as "Merrhis," "Pharos," "Muthidis," and on these, as well as other grounds, Mr. Paine (*Century Magazine*, May 1887) identifies her with "Nefarari Mer-en-mut" (beloved of Mut), who was both daughter (sister ?) and queen-consort of Rameses II.—one of the three whose names are recorded upon his monuments.

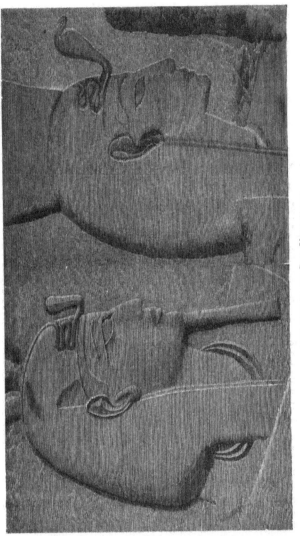

MENEPHTAH AND SETI MENEPHTAH.

some claim to the sovereignty; and this is offered
as the explanation of the passage in Hebrews,
"*Moses, when he was come to years, refused to be
called the son of Pharaoh's daughter; choosing
rather to suffer affliction with the people of God,
than to enjoy the pleasures of sin for a season*"
(xi. 24, 25). But such speculations cannot, I
think, be regarded as otherwise than idle.

The name of Moses does not appear either in
the numerous Papyri of the time, or on the
monuments of the Ramesside kings; and the
Exodus, when mentioned by ancient writers,
figures almost always as the expulsion of an un-
clean, leprous, or unseemly race, whose "existence
was displeasing to the Sun."[1]

We are here concerned, not with the casual
references to it which Josephus may have invented or preserved, but with the influence of
Egypt upon the Israelites, and (as the Israelites
were mainly a religious people[2]) mainly with its
influence upon their religious life.

[1] Lysimachus, Cory's *Fragments*, 185.
[2] "The great Semitic nations have been great along single
lines, excelling in one thing; in commerce like the Phoenicians,
religion like the Hebrews, war like the Arabs."—Fairbairn
Phil. of Religion and History, 262.

H

This influence was twofold : it produced imitation, and it also produced a reaction.

The minutiæ of the Mosaic law — the Ten Commandments themselves, which were possibly derived from the Confession before Osiris in the Book of the Dead,[1]—the Ark, the Shewbread, the institution of a Priesthood, all arose from what was dimly known to the captive Israelites of the religion of Egypt. But it must be remembered that, even in the case of Moses, this was probably but little. The deity "is not graven in marble, he is not beheld," say the *Records* (iv. 109). He is the " creator of kings, himself a mystery to men and gods" (vi. 24).

Herodotus, that most communicative of inquirers, speaks briefly and with awe of Osiris, " whose name I refrain from mentioning," and of the mysteries concerning which nothing " shall pass my lips " (ii. 171, 3). The gods of Egypt were, in fact, mysterious and unapproachable ; their worship could be practised only by the

[1] See also the maxims of Ptah - hotep, contained in the famous Prisse Papyrus. This has been called the "oldest book in the world." It dates from the XIIth dynasty, and is copied from a yet more ancient document (Edwards, *Pharaohs*, 220).

initiated; mystery was their favourite attribute, just as the plan of their temples was in such manner devised as to lead gradually from the full sunshine of the outer world to the obscurity of their retreat.[1]

"De la religion égyptienne," says Renan, "les Israélites ne connurent ainsi que le dehors, des momeries, des fétiches. Le dieu serpent les poursuivit durant des siècles, à la fois cauchemar et talisman" (i. 146).

It was when newly come out of Egypt that Aaron first, and Jeroboam in later days, set up the golden calf, in imitation of the sacred bull Apis, whom the Memphites worshipped, and said to the people, *Behold thy gods, O Israel, which brought thee up out of the land of Egypt.*[2] And it was after the sojourn in Egypt, too, that *God spake unto Moses and said unto him, I am Jehovah: I appeared unto Abraham, Isaac, and Jacob by the name of El Shaddai (God Almighty), but by my*

[1] Maspéro, *Eg. Arch.* 69.

[2] Exodus xxxii.; 1 Kings xii. Sir G. Wilkinson, however, says that "the offerings, dancings, and rejoicings practised on the occasion were doubtless in imitation of a ceremony they had witnessed in honour of Mnevis" (*Ancient Egyptians*, v. 197), the sacred beast of Heliopolis.

name Jehovah was I not known to them (Ex. vi. 2, 3).

In this narrowing down of El Elohim, God of the Universe,[1] to Jehovah, the tribal god of the Hebrews,—a god who loved Israel and hated the rest of the world, a god who competed almost upon equal terms with the *gods of Egypt*,—we trace the sinister influence of the Egyptian religion upon the Israelitish faith. "Le progrès religieux d'Israël consistera," says Renan, "à revenir de Iahvé à Élohim" (i. 86).

Not until the instinctive monotheism, which was, as it were, the birthright of the Jews, had suppressed the name Jehovah by declaring it too sacred to be spoken; not until the prophets had put before God's chosen people the true conception of the Lord of Heaven and Earth, was the victory won which gave life to the Jewish faith. *More than a prophet* was needed to prepare the way for Him who came into the world to bear witness of the Father's love; but it was by the

---

[1] The form of the name (a plural noun, though followed by a verb in the singular) is, says Dean Stanley, "at once the proof that monotheism rose on the ruins of a polytheistic faith, and that it absorbed and acknowledged the better tendencies of that faith" (i. 19).

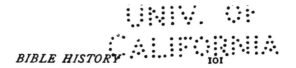

mouth of God's prophets that Israel was told *He
hath shewed thee, O man, what is good; and what
doth the Lord require of thee, but to do justly, and
to love mercy, and to walk humbly with thy God?* [1]

And this brings us to the second point of view
from which we must regard the influence of the
sojourn in Egypt upon the religion of the Israelites.

The laws of Moses were, says Manetho, "such
as were mainly opposite to the customs of the
Egyptians." And perhaps that Egyptian custom
which would have struck a stranger most, in
the days of the Ramesside kings, was the way
in which the dim phantoms of the future beyond the grave overshadowed the thought and
the art of the living present. The cheerful
pictures of joyous daily life, such as are to be
seen on the xiith dynasty tombs of Benihassan,
have altogether disappeared. "The dead is no
more to be seen at home, in the midst of his family.
. . . All has become, so to speak, fantastic and
chimerical." [2]

---

[1] Micah vi. 8 ; Hosea vi. 6 ; Amos v. 21 ; Matthew xi. 10 ;
John i. 23.

[2] Mariette, *Monuments of Upper Egypt*, 236—speaking, for
instance, of the tomb of Seti, near Thebes, commonly called
Belzoni's tomb.

The reception of the soul in the regions of the dead, its trial and judgment before Osiris, form the subject of thousands of exquisite sculptures and papyri.

"Delicate and sumptuous" as was the Egyptian's mode of life, beautiful, refined, and costly as were his house and furniture, it was yet upon the chambers which he built away to the West of his earthly home, in the desolate region where the sun ended its daily course, that the best efforts of his artificers were expended; so that those who travel to-day in the Land of Tombs still receive the impression which pervades Scripture history, and do not wonder that the Israelites, when they saw the Pharaoh in pursuit, cried out in bitter irony to Moses, "*Because there were no graves in Egypt, hast thou taken us away to die in the wilderness?*" (Ex. xiv. 11).

"For," says Diodorus, "the inhabitants of this country little value the short time of this present life, but put an high esteem upon the name and reputation of a virtuous life after death; and they call the houses of the living hostelries, because they stay in them but a little while; but the sepulchres of the dead they call everlasting habita-

tions, because they abide in the graves to infinite
generations.   Therefore they are not very curious
in the building of their houses; but in beautifying
their sepulchres they leave nothing undone that
can be thought of" (i. 4).

"When a man dies," he adds, "the friends and
nearest relations of the dead acquaint the judges
and the rest of their friends with the time pre-
fixed for the funeral of such a one by name,
declaring that such a day he is to pass the lake,
at which time forty judges appear and sit together
in a semicircle, in a place beyond the lake ; where
a ship (before provided by such as have the care
of the business) is haled up to the shore, governed
by a pilot whom the Egyptians call Charon.   And
therefore they say that Orpheus, seeing this ceremony when he was in Egypt, invented the fable
of Hell, partly imitating them in Egypt, and partly
adding something of his own. . . . The ship being
now in the lake, every one is at liberty by the law
to accuse the dead before the coffin be put aboard ;
and if any accuser appears, and makes good his
accusation that he lived an ill life, then the judges
give sentence, and the body is debarred from being
buried after the usual manner; but . . . if no

informer appear, or that the information prove
false, all the kindred of the deceased leave off
mourning and begin to set forth his praises "
(i. 7).

But this ceremony, whatever once its value
and meaning, grew to be merely a matter of
form. And though the Egyptians were, after
their manner, " religious," says Herodotus, " to
excess, far beyond any other race of men," we
cannot wonder that Moses, knowing little of the
hidden beauties of their belief, seeing only the
corruption, the cruelty, the callousness to every
virtue with which this intense religious sentiment
could be associated, determined to preach a very
different doctrine. It has often been remarked
that there is in the books of Moses no expression
of any thought, of any hope, of a life beyond the
grave : it may well be that this teaching was the
reaction from a system of religion where the belief
in a future state was so strong, and led, in the
present, to so little that was good.

And further,

> " The will
> Of the great gods is plain ; and ye must bring
> Ill deeds, ill passions, zealous to fulfil
> Their pleasure, to their feet."—ARNOLD.

The gods of Egypt, as known to their captives, were corrupt, lustful, cruel. The God of Moses, *a God of truth, and without iniquity, just and right is he.*

If thou wilt *do that which is right* (Ex. xv. 26), *if ye will obey my voice indeed, and keep my covenant, then ye shall be a peculiar treasure unto me above all people* (xix. 5). *If ye walk in my statutes, and keep my commandments, and do them ; then . . . I will walk among you, and will be your God, and ye shall be my people* (Lev. xxvi. 3, 12)—this was the message that Moses had to give.

"*For I spake not unto your fathers,*" says Jeremiah, "*nor commanded them in the day that I brought them out of the land of Egypt, concerning burnt offerings or sacrifices : but this thing commanded I them, saying, Obey my voice, and I will be your God, and ye shall be my people : and walk ye in all the ways that I have commanded you, that it may be well with you*" (vii. 22).

For this commandment, says the writer of Deuteronomy, *which I command thee this day, it is not hidden from thee, neither is it far off. It is not in heaven, that thou shouldest say, Who shall go up for us to heaven, and bring it unto us, that we may hear*

*it, and do it?   Neither is it beyond the sea, that
thou shouldest say, Who shall go over the sea for us,
and bring it unto us, that we may hear it, and do
it?   But the word is very nigh unto thee, in thy
mouth, and in thy heart, that thou mayest do it.
See, I have set before thee this day life and good, and
death and evil; in that I command thee this day to
love the Lord thy God, to walk in his ways, and to
keep his commandments and his statutes and his
judgments, that thou mayest live and multiply*
(xxx. 11-16).

And so Israel became the bringer in and
defender of the idea of Conduct, "the lifter up
to the nations of the banner of Righteousness."
Righteousness was their religion: *the secret of
the Lord was with them* (Ps. xxv. 14).

"This does truly constitute for Israel a most
extraordinary distinction.   In spite of all which
in them and in their character is unattractive,
nay, repellent,—in spite of their shortcomings
even in righteousness itself and their insignificance
in everything else,—this petty, unsuccessful, un-
amiable people, without politics, without science,
without art, without charm, deserve their great
place in the world's regard, and are likely to have

it more, as the world goes on, rather than less.
It is secured to them by the facts of human nature,
and by the unalterable constitution of things.
'God hath given commandment to bless, and he
hath blessed, and we cannot reverse it; he hath
not seen iniquity in Jacob, and he hath not seen
perverseness in Israel; the Eternal, his God is
with him!'" [1]

NOTE.—In 1881 a wonderful discovery was made at Deir-
el-bahari, on the left bank of the Nile, near Thebes. There
were discovered the actual mummies, the embalmed
bodies, of the Pharaohs of the Bondage and the Exodus,
together with many others of interest hardly less absorb-
ing.   For several years M. Maspéro, then the Director-
General of the Boulak Museum at Cairo, had noticed the
number of valuable relics which were offered for sale by
the Arabs at Thebes, and had suspected that these knew
the secret of some royal tombs as yet unexplored by
science.   For a long time no rewards, no threats or
punishments, availed to extract the secret; but at last, in
the summer of 1881, it was discovered.   Herr Emil
Brugsch hurried at once to Thebes; and there, in a small
cave among the western hills, he beheld the mummies of
no less than thirty-six kings and queens and priests, with
beautiful mummy cases, gold and silver ornaments, priceless papyri, all lying huddled together in bewildering
confusion.

[1] Arnold, *Literature and Dogma*, 42, 205.

The mummies found included those of King Rasekenen or Ta-āken, and of Aahmes I., the founders of the
xvIIIth dynasty; and also of Ne-fert-ari Aahmes,
whose name means "the beautiful consort of Aahmes,"
ancestress of the new empire. Belonging to the
xvIIIth dynasty, too, were Amenhotep I., Thothmes II.,
and the illustrious Thothmes III. ; and with them, en-
closed in a beautifully inlaid casket, the intestines of the
woman-king Hatasou. There were also Seti I. of the
xIxth dynasty, and his son the great Rameses ; the xxth
dynasty Rameses III., last of the great warrior-kings of
Egypt ; and some of the Queens and Priest-kings of the
xxIst dynasty.

These were all brought to the surface and carried, in
weird procession, under the broiling July sun, across the
plain to the river-bank, thence to be conveyed down the
Nile to Cairo, where they now lie in the museum of the
Ghizeh Palace. (*Century Magazine*, May 1887 ; Robinson, *Pharaohs of Bondage and Exodus* ; Brugsch, *Egypt*,
131, 359, new ed. ; St. Clair, *Buried Cities*, 22 ; Stuart
Poole, *Cities of Egypt*, 63.)

CHAPTER III

"Say unto Tyrus, O thou that art situate at the entry of the sea, and which art a merchant of the people for many isles." —Ezek. xxvii. 3.

"Is this your joyous city, whose antiquity is of ancient days? her own feet shall carry her afar off to sojourn. Who hath taken this counsel against Tyre, the crowning city, whose merchants are princes, whose traffickers are the honourable of the earth? The Lord of hosts hath purposed it, to stain the pride of all glory, and to bring into contempt all the honourable of the earth." —Is. xxiii. 7-9.

DURING their sojourn in Egypt, the Israelites had been in contact with a highly civilised nation, from whose monuments and records many side-lights are shed upon their history. But after the Exodus, in the days when *there was no king in Israel*, we pass on to a time during which no intercourse took place between the Hebrews and any people whose monuments we can decipher.

With the Hittites, indeed, they had relations, and the statement in the Book of Joshua (xi. 4) that

this people had *horses and chariots very many* is
confirmed by the Egyptian monuments, which show
us that just at this time the Hittites were at the
height of their power, and that in their chariots
lay their chiefest strength.   It has been shown now,
too, that the Hittites were no petty tribe of
Canaan, but a great people who once ruled from the
Euphrates to the Aegean Sea : and thus the Bible
references to their power are amply vindicated.
But as yet their inscriptions are a sealed book to
us. We must wait for fresh light from the Hittite
monuments until we have the key to their decipher-
ment—until Kirjath Sepher, the " Book-town " of
the Hittites, is disinterred, or until the tomb of
the beautiful Hittite wife of Rameses II. is discovered, and with it, perhaps, the " silver tablet "
on which Khita-sira, her father, had inscribed his
version of the treaty with the great Pharaoh.
(See p. 81.)

Meanwhile we know that after the time of
Menephtah the decline of Egypt became very
rapid. When the great and powerful xixth
dynasty had come to its inglorious end, there
followed, indeed, another Theban line of kings,

headed by a monarch as mighty as any that had gone before — Rameses III., whose name, Ramessu-Pa-netu ("Rameses the god"), formed the well-known Rhampsinitus of Greek historians.

The great Harris Papyrus, one of the finest, best written, and best preserved that have been discovered in Egypt, is entirely devoted to the praises of Rameses III., and to the commemoration of "the good and glorious works which he performed to the men of the land of Egypt, and of every land assembled together at one time ; to inform the fathers, the gods and goddesses of the south and north, mortals, intelligences, mankind, of the numerous glorious actions which he did on earth while great Ruler of Egypt."

"I am king on earth, ruler of the living," he says to Amen, his god ; "I made for thee a noble house . . . filling its treasury with the products of the land of Egypt, gold, silver, and all precious stones for hundreds of thousands ; its granaries had their heaps of corn and barley, its fields and herds multiplied like the sands of the shore" (*Rec.* vi. 23-26).

The list of the treasures accumulated—gold and silver, spices and jewels, fine linen and provisions of food,—detailed upon the Papyrus, curiously confirms the account of Herodotus, that "King Rhampsinitus was possessed, they said, of great riches in silver, — indeed to such an amount, that none of the Princes, his successors, surpassed or even equalled his wealth. . . . The same king, I was also informed by the priests, afterwards descended alive into the region which the Greeks call Hades, and there played at dice with Ceres, sometimes winning, and sometimes suffering defeat."[1]   The great temple at Medinet-Abou, where gold and silver vases are portrayed upon the walls, recalls, too, the "vast chamber of hewn stone" built by Rhampsinitus.   It shows, more-over, that architecture did not follow engraving and sculpture in their rapid downfall, for the temple is one of the most remarkable in Egypt.

Rameses III. was a great conqueror, as well as a powerful and wealthy ruler.   "Thus have I taken from the nations the desire to direct their thoughts against Egypt," grimly says the record upon his temple of victory.

But though his reign forms a bright page in the

---

[1] ii. 121. Hades was the Egyptian Amenti, presided over by Osiris and Isis (the Ceres of Herodotus).

history of his country, Egyptian power, like Egyptian art, was already on the wane. With Rameses III. closes the glorious period of Egyptian

MUMMY HEAD OF PAI-NET'EM II.

history; and during the XXIst dynasty the royal power passed into the hands of a succession of military pontiffs or priest-kings, who exerted little or no influence upon the fortunes of the nations round.

I

One of them, probably Pai-net'em II., was the Pharaoh who *made affinity with* Solomon (1 Kings iii. 1), and gave him his daughter in marriage.

His mummy was among those found in 1881 at Deir-el-Bahari. Among them also was the mummy of one of the queens of the dynasty, Ma-ka-ra; and with her a small queen only 16 inches long, a little coiled-up bundle of a baby, lying at its mother's feet, that, dying before it saw the light, yet figures on the official papyrus in the coffin as " queen Maut-em-hat," " royal daughter, royal wife, royal mother "—nay, even " principal royal spouse." [1]

Meanwhile Assyria, hitherto held in check by Egyptian conquerors, profited by the decay of Egypt to make herself mistress of northern Syria; and under Tiglath-Pileser I., whose reign (1120-1100 B.C.) forms an era in Assyrian history, she had become the foremost monarchy of the world. But after his death and that of his son she relapsed

---

[1] St. Clair, *Buried Cities*, 27 ; Robinson, *Pharaohs of Bondage and Exodus*, 47 (in a chapter quaintly entitled " The Mummies as Evidences of Christianity "). The *t'* in Pai-net'em should be pronounced like a hard *ch* (Brugsch, *Egypt*, viii. new ed. 1891).

into obscurity; the very names of her sovereigns are unknown to us, and for a period of 150 years the only Assyrian inscription extant is a record of disaster to the Assyrian arms.

It is during this interval, when both the great neighbouring nations were passing through a period of obscurity—the interval between the decline of Assyria, 1100 B.C., and the recovery of Egypt under Shishak, 990 B.C.—that Scripture history places the empire of David and Solomon; and it is during this interval alone that such an empire could have existed. At no other time would the little State have been allowed to extend her borders and develop her resources without interference, without being overwhelmed by one or other of her powerful neighbours, or crushed to powder between the two. Never before, and never after, did she take her place among the great monarchies of the East; but now, for a brief period, lasting all told only seventy years, she was to become the mistress of an empire stretching from the river Euphrates to the border of Egypt, from the Mediterranean to the Gulf of Akaba, and receiving annual tribute from many subject princes.

This empire of David and Solomon is chiefly known to us for its might and magnificence, for its splendour and success. But its main interest lies, perhaps, in the fact that it brought the Children of Israel into contact with one of the most interesting and remarkable of the peoples of the ancient world. *And Hiram king of Tyre*, we read, *sent his servants unto Solomon ; for he had heard that they had anointed him king in the room of his father : for Hiram was ever a lover of David* (1 Kings v. 1).

The inhabitants of Tyre—the Phoenicians, or Canaanites of earlier Bible history—were, says Renan, a branch of the same great race as the Hebrews — a family who, "sortie la première du berceau commun de la race sémitique," had early become civilised, and in devoting their energies to commerce and luxury had become objects of hatred to their shepherd kinsfolk. [1]

That the Phoenicians and Canaanites were identical is amply proved. "The Septuagint frequently renders Canaan and Canaanite in the Hebrew by Phoenicia and Phoenician, and even

[1] Renan, *Langues Sém.* i. 176.

the Carthaginians in their African settlements called themselves Canaanites. The woman whom the Evangelist Mark (vii. 26), writing, as is commonly supposed, for Gentile readers, calls a Syrophoenician, Matthew (xv. 22), addressing his own countrymen, probably in their own language, calls a Canaanite. But the most decisive proof is furnished by a Phoenician coin, which bears the inscription ‘Laodicea, Mother in Canaan.’ ”[1]

The Phoenicians are the people to whom the world owes the knowledge of alphabetic writing. Prof. Sayce thinks that, settled in the Delta in the time of the Hyksos kings, they borrowed the alphabet from their Egyptian neighbours, and thence handed it on to the mother country. Here the letters were called by names derived from the shapes which they resembled, or from things whose names began with sounds they represented; and

---

[1] Kenrick, *Phoenicia*, 42. The coin is of the age of Antiochus, IV. Epiphanes.

St. Augustine says that the peasants in the western part of North Africa derived themselves from fugitives expelled from Palestine by “Joshua the son of Nun, the Plunderer.” “Interrogati rustici nostri quid sint, Punicé respondentes ‘Canani,’ ” he says, adding that to be accurate they should have said “Chanani” (*Dict. of Bible*, “Phoenicia”; Rawlinson, *Hist. Ill.* 86).

these names have been passed on to us through the Greeks. The very word Alphabet is a memorial of the fact, since it is composed of *alpha* and *beta*, the Greek names of the two first letters, which, in their turn, are simply the Phoenician *aleph*, an ox, and *beth*, a house.[1]

But it is a curious fact that this people—who during long ages were the only intermediaries between the Semitic races and the rest of the civilised world, who transmitted to the other nations, even if they did not invent, the art of alphabetic writing—left no written records of their history, not the smallest fragment of literature. From the Jews, therefore, who alone among the Semitic races preserved records for posterity before the second century B.C., we learn almost all that we know about the Phoenicians; and it is in the light of the bitter national hatred between Israel and Canaan that the latter appear to us. "In judging of the national character by the language of the Jewish writers, we must remember," says Kenrick, "that we are reading the words of national rivals, to whom Phoenicia was a 'pricking brier and a grieving thorn.'" "It must not be forgotten,"

[1] Sayce, *Fresh Light*, 86, 87.

he adds, "that the shrewdness of a commercial nation appears in the invidious light of fraud to those who feel themselves at disadvantage in dealing with them. The Dutch in their mercantile character were hated and contemned by the rest of Europe, at the time when Holland was conspicuous for valour, industry, learning, and religion." [1]

We must not judge of the Canaanites out of the mouths of their enemies, just as we must not take too literally the expression "Punica fides" with which the Romans stamped upon history their view of their Phoenician rivals at Carthage.

The wisdom and enterprise of the Phoenician cities appear, indeed, everywhere in the chronicles of their enemies—in the scornful reference of Zechariah to *Zidon, though it be very wise* (ix. 2), as in the bitterly ironical praises of Ezekiel, addressing the prince of Tyre. "*Behold, thou art wiser than Daniel,*" he says ; "*there is no secret that they can hide from thee : with thy wisdom and with thine understanding thou hast gotten thee riches, and hast gotten gold and silver into thy treasures : by thy great wisdom, and by thy traffick, hast thou increased thy riches*" (xxviii. 3-5).

[1] Kenrick, *Phoenicia*, 279.

In the earliest times of which the knowledge has come down to us, Sidon, whose name is the Greek form of the Phoenician Zidon, The Fisheries—Sidon, the *firstborn of Canaan*—was supreme among the Phoenician cities. She became "*great Zidon*" when, after the death of Rameses II., the dominion in Canaan had slipped from the hands of his successors; and she is often mentioned in Homer as well as in the book of Joshua, while Tyre, her "daughter," appears only once in Joshua and never in Homer. After the taking of Sidon by the Philistine king of Ascalon in the latter half of the thirteenth century B.C., Tyre became supreme; and though the exact date of the event is uncertain, the fact itself is one of the few which have been distinctly preserved to us in early Phoenician history.[1]

"But we have no connected history of Tyre till near the age of Solomon, whose relations with Hiram induced Josephus to extract some passages from the Tyrian histories of Dius and Menander. Before this time we have only mythic names."[2]

---

[1] Justin says that the taking of Sidon, and the migration of her inhabitants to Tyre, occurred the year before the taking of Troy. Kenrick, *Phoenicia*, 342.

[2] Kenrick, *Phoenicia*, 346, 85. See also Rawlinson, *Phoenicia*, 406, etc.

Phoenix, the father of Cadmus and Europa, is the country of Phoenicia; and Cadmus (*Kedem*, the east), seeking to discover Europa (*Ereb*, the west),[1] is merely the history of Phoenician colonisation "brought into that compact and personal form which Greek mythology loved to give to vague and remote tradition."

Hiram and his predecessor Abibaal are, indeed, historical personages; and long before their time the trade of Phoenicia was already encircling the world. She had settlements in Cyprus, in Crete, in Spain; she had brought tin from Britain[2] and amber from the Baltic shores; already her very name had come, in the Semitic dialects, to mean trader, or pedlar.

"*She maketh fine linen, and selleth it; she delivereth girdles to the Canaanite,*" says the Book of Proverbs (xxxi. 24), describing the virtuous woman. "*Ephraim is a Canaanite; the balances of*

---

[1] Ereb is the same as Erebus, darkness; whence also the name Arab, given to the dwellers in the westernmost parts of Asia (Rawlinson, *Herodotus*, ii. p. 83).

[2] We are, says Sir J. Lubbock, "quite justified in concluding that between 1500 B.C. and 1200 B.C. the Phoenicians were already acquainted with the mineral fields of Spain and Britain." —*Prehistoric Times*, 69.

deceit are in his hand," says Hosea (xii. 7) of his money-loving country ; while Isaiah appears to use the term in a nobler sense when he speaks of *Tyre, the city that dispenseth crowns, whose merchants are princes, whose Canaanites are the honoured of the land* (xxiii. 8).

Very famous, too, were her manufactures.

Pliny tells the story current in his day as to the discovery of glass—how that some merchants, who were carrying a cargo of natron (used in Syria for soap [1]), having gone ashore near Accho to cook their dinner, had propped their cauldron for lack of stones on lumps of natron, which, being melted by the heat, became mixed with the fine white sand, "and they beheld transparent streams flowing forth, of a liquid hitherto unknown ; this, it is said, was the origin of glass." [2]

The story is probably apocryphal; and in any case glass was known in Egypt before 2000 B.C., for upon the XIIth dynasty tombs of Benihassan there are paintings of glass-blowers at work. But it is certain that the manufacture of glass was

---

[1] Jer. ii. 22, *" though thou wash thee with nitre, and take thee much sope."*

[2] Pliny, *Nat. Hist.* bk. 36, ch. 65.

from very early times the characteristic industry of Sidon.

And

> " Who has not heard how Tyrian shells
>   Enclosed the blue, that dye of dyes,
> Whereof one drop worked miracles,
>   And coloured like Astarte's eyes
> Raw silk the merchant sells ? "

To this day are to be seen along the Syrian coast huge mounds formed of the refuse of the Murex [1] shells, whence Phoenician manufacturers had extracted the dye that was one of the glories of their commerce—the " imperial purple " which, later, Roman emperors tried, by sumptuary laws, to restrict to their own use.

Thus did Tyre *suck of the abundance of the seas, and of treasures hid in the sand* (Deut. xxxiii. 19). Already, too, she was celebrated for her exquisite work in metal and precious stones, in silk and fine linen. And the vessels which the skilful Tyrian workman made for Solomon's temple were probably not less artistic than the beautifully embossed metal work which General di Cesnola has found on the island of Cyprus.

---

[1] *Murex trunculus*, and *brandaris*.   Lortet, *La Syrie d'aujourdhui*, 102.

Homer tells how the maidens of the Greek isles were captivated by the trinkets which the cunning workers of Tyre loved to make and to sell. The vase offered by Achilles as a prize in the funeral games in honour of Patroclus, was a work of the skilful Sidonians; and the bowl of silver which Menelaus gave to Telemachus had been a gift to him from their king; while among the spoils which Paris brought home with him to Troy, after his wanderings with Helen, were "robes, many coloured, the work of Sidonian women." [1]

Another and a darker trade had the Phoenicians, too, with Greece. The Eumaeus of Homer is kidnapped and sold as a slave by " crafty Phoenicians." Ulysses narrowly escapes the same fate. " *The children also of Judah and the children of Jerusalem have ye sold unto the Grecians,*" cries Joel (iii. 6) —the first of the prophets who inveighed against Tyre; and Amos, his contemporary, re-echoes the reproach (i. 9, ii. 6).

The luxury of Tyre, her corruption, *the multitude of* her *merchandise, the iniquity of* her

---

[1] *Iliad,* vi. 290-292 ; quoted in Rawlinson's *Herodotus,* ii. 188. See Kenrick, *Phoenicia,* 341, 189; Rawlinson, *Phoenicia,* 408.

traffick (Ezek. xxviii. 16, 18), her *riches and* her *fairs,'* her *merchandise and* her *mariners* (xxvii. 27), form the theme of bitter denunciation by prophet after prophet. That she should *no more rejoice*; that the *pride of her glory should be stained* (Is. xxiii.); that Tyrus who *did build herself a stronghold, and heaped up silver as the dust, and fine gold as the mire of the streets,* should be *devoured with fire,* became their longing anticipation. *"Thus saith the Lord God; Behold, I am against thee, O Zidon,"* was the cry of Ezekiel (xxviii. 22); and *"Is this your joyous city, whose antiquity is of ancient days?"* was the exultant taunt of Isaiah (xxiii. 7).

"A mournful and solitary silence now prevails along the shore, which once resounded with the world's debate." Tyre has become *a place for the spreading of nets in the midst of the sea* (Ezek. xxvi. 5). But in the days of Solomon, as in the days of the prophets, she was *"the mart of nations," "the crowning city," "merchant of the people for many isles."* And Ezekiel could give no more graphic picture of her commerce than by representing her as the mistress of the sea, seated amidst its waters, under the emblem of one of

her own beautiful state galleys, with cedar from
Lebanon for masts, with row-benches of box from
Chittim, inlaid with ivory, with sails made of
fine linen with broidered work from Egypt, and an
awning of her own imperial purple (xxvii.).

The Phoenician cities, *situate at the entrance
of the sea* (Ezek. xxvii. 3) on the narrow strip of
coast line between the Mediterranean and the
mountains of Lebanon, whose enchanted pleasure-
grounds, bubbling with fountains and carpeted by
flowers, were divided from one another by deep
clefts and precipices, naturally produced a sea-
faring population. Handling with skill their Sea-
horses (as the name they gave to their vessels signifies), the Phoenicians rode from shore to shore.

Up to the time of David they had been
absolutely the only intermediaries between Syria
and the outer world; for their neighbours and
kinsfolk, the Children of Israel, had possessed no
harbour, no point of vantage upon the sea-coast.
But David's conquest of Edom (2 Sam. viii. 14)
had given his people not only a port, *Ezion-geber,
which is beside Eloth, on the shore of the Red Sea*
(1 Kings ix. 26), but the command of the trade with
the far East, which enabled him to strike a bargain

with the jealous merchant people who were his
neighbours; for the Phoenicians had no port upon
the Red Sea.[1]   To Ezion-geber travelled King
Solomon himself, to superintend the making of
his fleet. _ Manned by Phoenician sailors, *shipmen,
that had knowledge of the sea,* his vessels, taking
part in the trade of the East, *came to Ophir,*[2] *and
fetched from thence gold, and brought it to king
Solomon.*

[1] Ewald, *Hist.* iii. 263.

[2] Ophir, originally supposed to be Malabar (Renan, *Lang.
Sém.* i. 194), is now considered to be the mouth of the Indus
(*Hist. d'Israel*, ii. 119).

"The evidence seems to me," says Professor Max Müller,
"to incline in favour of India, or of a seaport on the south-east
coast of Arabia, carrying on an active trade with India.   The
names for *algum trees,* as well as for *apes, peacocks,* and *ivory,*
are foreign words in Hebrew. . . . If, therefore, we can find a
language, in which the name for *algum tree* . . . is indigenous,
we may be certain that the country in which that language
was spoken must have been the country from whence Solomon
obtained algum trees, and, therefore, the Ophir of the Bible. . . .
Now, *apes* are called in Hebrew *Koph,* a word without an
etymology in the Semitic languages, but nearly identical in
sound with the Sanscrit name of ape, *Kapi.*" — *Lectures on
the Science of Language,* i. 231-233, 1871.

On the other hand, if the much-talked-of remains in Mashona-
land turn out to be really Phoenician, the theory that South
Africa is the Bible Ophir will have received strong support.
See *Times,* 23rd July ; *Spectator,* 25th July, 1891.

Then, too, came about that first historic contact between West and East, which has so powerfully impressed the imagination of mankind. *The kings of Tarshish and of the isles shall bring presents* from the West, sang the Psalmist; *the kings of Sheba and Seba shall offer gifts* from the East. *Yea,* ALL KINGS *shall fall down before him:* ALL NATIONS *shall serve him* (Ps. lxxii.).

For the discovery of Tarshish was to the Phoenicians very much what the discovery of the New World was to the Spaniards and the English of the sixteenth century. There, said the ancients, was the boundary line of night and day; there Helios kept his flocks and herds; there Orthros (the Dawn) fed the oxen of Hades.

To Tarshish, the modern Andalusia, the fertile plain through which flows the Guadalquivir, sailed the newly formed fleet of Solomon, to return with *silver, iron, tin, and lead* (Ezek. xxvii. 12), which are the productions of Tartessus, mentioned in all classical writers.

Silver, in particular, was there so plentiful that, according to Diodorus, when "in ancient time a mountain tract was set on fire by some shepherds, which continued burning for many days together (whence the mountains were called Pyrenaean, *fiery*), the parched superficies of the earth sweated abundance of silver, and the ore being melted, the metal flowed down in streams of pure silver like a river : the use whereof being unknown to the inhabitants, the Phoenician merchants bought it for trifles given for it in exchange; and by transporting it into Greece, Asia, and all other nations, greatly enriched themselves. And such was their covetousness, that when they had fully loaded their ships, and had much more silver to bring aboard, they cut off the lead from their anchors, and made use of silver instead " (v. 2).

And all king Solomon's drinking vessels were of gold, and all the vessels of the house of the forest of Lebanon were of pure gold, says the writer of Kings ; *none were of silver: it was nothing accounted of in the days of Solomon* (1 Kings x. 21).

Once in three years came the navy of Tarshish,[1]

---

[1] The author of the book of Chronicles, copying 1 Kings x. 22, supposes that the expression *ships of Tarshish* meant ships sailing to Tarshish. But obviously "the words had come to signify large Phoenician ships, of a particular size and description, destined for long voyages, just as in English 'East Indiaman' was a general name given to vessels, some of which were not intended to go to India at all" (*Dict. of Bible*). See also Renan, *Hist. d'Israel*, ii. 120, "navire transatlantique." The

K

bringing gold, and silver, ivory, and apes, and pea-cocks—things beautiful and strange to the eyes of a hitherto untravelled people, Indian products whose very names in Hebrew are but adaptations from the Sanscrit of the lands from which they came.

And besides this commerce by sea, with Spain, India, and the coasts of Africa, there was also commerce by land, not only with Tyre herself, but with Egypt and Arabia. It was in connection with this commerce that, in Solomon's reign, was founded the Khan or Caravanserai of Chimham, *which is by Bethlehem*, the starting-point whence men still went *to enter into Egypt* in the days of Jeremiah (xli. 17); and, "considering the stationary character of all Eastern institutions, we may well believe," says Canon Farrar, "that it was in the stable of that caravanserai that the Christ was born."

Solomon's alliance with Egypt, signalised by his splendid marriage with the daughter of the

mention of peacocks in 1 Kings x. 22 shows that this interpretation is the right one, for peacocks were only found in India. See also 1 Kings xxii. 48, *Jehoshaphat made ships of Tarshish to go to Ophir for gold*, while Chronicles has it *to go to Tarshish* (2 Chron. xx. 36).

Pharaoh,[1] was the first step in that new policy which was to lead Israel so far from the path of her true progress. " When Solomon married the daughter of Pharaoh," says the Talmud, " Gabriel descended and fixed a reed in the sea. A sand-bank formed around it, upon which the mighty city of Rome was subsequently built."

The change was typified by that importation of chariots and *horses brought out of Egypt*, which belonged to an aggressive rather than to a defensive foreign policy.

Up to that time the horse, the emblem of the pride and power of the heathen nations,[2] had been almost unused in Israel. David's sons, Absalom and Adonijah, had, it is true, in their presumptuous extravagance, *prepared them chariots and*

---

[1] The traditional interpretation refers the forty-fifth Psalm, "the Song of Loves," to this marriage ; but Delitzsch thinks it was occasioned by the marriage of Athaliah with Joram, the son of Jehoshaphat, the " second Solomon of Jewish history " ; and some critics have referred it to the marriage of Ahab and Jezebel (*Teacher's Prayer Book*).

[2] Note the curious touch in Judges—"*And the Lord was with Judah ; and he drave out the inhabitants of the mountains ; but could not drive out the inhabitants of the valley, because they had chariots of iron* " (i. 19). See also the acrimonious and *tu-quoque* defence of the Jews against the charge of worshipping the ass, by Josephus (Cont. App. ii. 7).

horsemen (2 Sam. xv. 1 ; 1 Kings i. 5), but David himself had always been wont to ride upon a mule. *" An horse is a vain thing for safety,"* said the Psalmist. Now, however, King Solomon *gathered together chariots and horsemen,* which were reckoned by the thousand; and special officers were appointed to oversee them. The change in the national feeling on this matter is typified in the despairing cry both of Elisha to Elijah, and of King Joash to Elisha himself, when each saw his people about to lose their best help and strength—*" O my father, my father, the chariot of Israel, and the horsemen thereof!"* (2 Kings ii. 12, and xiii. 14).

There came a time when the horse was again to the Israelites the emblem of conquest and invasion, and when their seers began to look for a king *lowly and riding upon an ass* (Zech. ix. 9).

But meanwhile Solomon's chariot, with its pillars of silver and its awning of purple, was one of the wonders of that sumptuous court, worthy to be compared (Cant. i. 9) to the beautiful Egyptian bride, who seems to have lent imagery to much of the poetry of the day.

. According to the tradition preserved by Josephus, it was the habit of the king to make his progresses about Jerusalem, clothed all in white, with an escort of noble youths, " in garments of Tyrian purple," whose long hair hanging down was sprinkled with dust of gold, "so that their heads sparkled with the reflection of the sunbeams " (viii. 7, 3).

"Who is this," cries the author of Canticles, breathing the spirit of the time, "who is this that cometh out of the wilderness like pillars of smoke, perfumed with myrrh and frankincense, with all powders of the merchant? Behold his litter, it is Solomon's ; threescore valiant men are about it, of the valiant of Israel. . . . King Solomon made himself a litter of the wood of Lebanon. He made the pillars thereof of silver, the bottom thereof of gold, the covering of it of purple, the midst thereof being paved with love, for the daughters of Jerusalem. Go forth, O ye daughters of Zion, and behold king Solomon with the crown wherewith his mother crowned him in the day of his espousals, and in the day of the gladness of his heart" (iii. 6-11).[1]

---

[1] To the contentment of that period, says Ewald, "we see in the Canticles a brilliant testimony, still preserved from the age immediately after Solomon " (*Hist.* iii. 265). He considers the Song of Songs an " undeniable Hebrew opera," a " kind of drama " (282). Renan agrees with Ewald as to its date, holding that it was written after the death of Solomon, but while Tirzah was still the northern capital, before Samaria was built (*Cant. des Cant.* 97-101). " Nous persistons donc," he says,

The king's passion was for magnificence. The beautiful temple which he built ; the house of the forest of Lebanon, its tall armoury glittering with shields like the bejewelled neck of the lovely bride (Cant. iv. 4) ; the porch or gate of judgment where (after the manner of all Eastern sovereigns) was placed the throne of judgment—the *great throne of ivory*, overlaid with gold, supported by the lions of Judah, of which *there was not the like made in any kingdom ; his ascent by which he went up into the house of the Lord ;* his towers and fortifications, summer palaces and stately gardens ; the equipment of his luxurious court ; the maintenance of his enormous harem, *and the meat of his table, and the sitting of his servants, and the attendance of his ministers, and their apparel, and his cupbearers* (1 Kings x. 5),—all, while he lived, dazzled and entranced his people, and remained, even in the time of Our Lord, the very sign and symbol of earthly glory (Matt. vi. 29).

"Il y a des heures," says Renan, "dans la vie la plus religieuse, où l'on fait une halte au bord de

---

"avec Herder, Ewald, etc., à placer la composition du Cantique des Cantiques peu de temps après le schisme, c'est à dire vers le milieu du xme siècle avant Jésus-Christ" (p. 111).

la route, et où l'on oublie les devoirs austères, pour s'amuser un moment, comme les femmes du sérail de Salomon, avec les perles et les perroquets d'Ophir " (ii. 137).

But these things marked a departure from the true traditions of the Israelitish race and faith. The destiny of Israel was to excel, not on the lines of industry, of commerce, or of war, but as the people who first grasped, and most firmly held, the great doctrine that to righteousness belongs salvation; that all men are equal at the judgment-seat of God.

The writer of Deuteronomy, who, two centuries after the time of Solomon, sang of his failure and of its causes, places first among them his turning aside from the way marked out for Israel.

" *He shall not multiply horses to himself, nor cause the people to return to Egypt, to the end that he should multiply horses,*" he says of the ideal king : "*forasmuch as the Lord hath said unto you, Ye shall henceforth return no more that way. Neither shall he multiply wives to himself, that his heart turn not away : neither shall he greatly multiply to himself silver and gold . . . that he may learn to fear the Lord his God. . . . That his heart be not lifted up above his brethren, and that he turn not aside from the commandment, to the right hand, or to the left: to the end that he may prolong his days in his kingdom, he, and his children, in the midst of Israel* " (Deut. xvii. 16-20).

" How wise wast thou in thy youth, and as a flood filled with understanding," says the Apocryphal writer. " Thy name went far into the islands . . . the countries marvelled at thee. Thou didst gather gold as tin, and didst multiply silver as lead. . . . But, by thy body thou wast brought into subjection. Thou didst stain thine honour, and pollute thy seed " (Ecclus. xlvii.).

But King Solomon loved many strange women, thus begins the record of his decline, *together with the daughter of Pharaoh, women of the Moabites, Ammonites, Edomites, Zidonians, and Hittites; . . . And it came to pass, when Solomon was old, that his wives turned away his heart after other gods: and his heart was not perfect with the Lord his God, as was the heart of David his father. For Solomon went after Ashtoreth the goddess of the Zidonians, and after Milcom the abomination of the Ammonites. . . . Then did Solomon build an high place for Chemosh, the abomination of Moab, in the hill that is before Jerusalem, and for Molech, the abomination of the children of Ammon. And likewise did he for all his strange wives, which burnt incense and sacrificed unto their gods.*—1 Kings xi. 1-8.

These were the chief of the "gods adored among

the nations round," whose seats Solomon, in his
idolatrous old age, fixed

> "next the seat of God . . .
> And with their darkness durst affront His light."

Of the horrid rites with which they were worshipped, many details have come down to us.

> "Moonèd Ashtaroth,
> Heaven's queen and mother both,"

—the moon, *the queen of heaven* (Jer. vii. 18),
the consort of the Sun-god Baal—was the goddess
whose impure and licentious worship was the
darkest blot on the Assyrian and Canaanitish
religions. To her were dedicated those *prophets
of the groves* who came to Samaria in the train of
Jezebel, the Tyrian princess. For Ahab *took to
wife Jezebel, the daughter of Ethbaal, king of the
Zidonians* (1 Kings xvi. 31), who reigned at Tyre
about half a century after the time of Hiram, and
who was himself, according to Josephus, a "priest
of Astarte."

The *prophets of Baal four hundred and fifty,
and the prophets of the groves four hundred,* which
ate at Jezebel's table in Samaria, still have their
counterparts in Eastern lands to-day. A recent

traveller in Tunis has described the religious
ceremony of a sect of dervishes, witnessed by
him at Kairwan, where "writhing and contorted
objects," delirious with religious frenzy, shrieking
aloud the praises of Allah, cut themselves with
long knives like cutlasses, or forced iron skewers
into their unresisting flesh, or greedily ate hand-
fuls of jagged glass; while "ever behind and
through all re-echoed the perpetual and pitiless
accompaniment of the drums," and the plaintive
quavering wail of Arab song.[1] Well may that
sickening scene have brought to his mind how the
prophets of Baal *cried aloud, and cut themselves
after their manner with knives and lancets, till the
blood gushed out upon them* (1 Kings xviii. 28).

Ashtoreth was, as we have seen, identical with
the Istar of the old Babylonian myths.   One of
the most poetic of these told how Istar had wedded
the young and beautiful Sun-god Samas, or Tammuz, only-begotten of the Night; and of her search
for him in Hades, when he was slain by the Boar's
tusk of Winter.   The Phoenician Semites kept
his festival, and the time of the summer solstice

---

[1] "Salvation by Torture at Kairwan," by Hon. G. N. Curzon,
M.P., *Fortnightly Review*, July 1887.

was to them the "month of Tammuz." Three centuries after Solomon had introduced the worship of Ashtoreth into Jerusalem, Ezekiel saw in his vision *the door of the gate of the Lord's house . . . and behold there sat women weeping for Tammuz* (viii. 14). And St. Jerome, writing in the fourth century of our own era, tells that "Bethlehem is now overshadowed by the grove of Tammuz, who is Adonis; and in the cave where Christ wailed as a Babe, the paramour of Venus now is mourned."[1]

Chemosh, the abomination of Moab, was the deity in whose honour was erected that curious "Moabite stone" which probably belongs to the time of Ahaziah, Ahab's son, and which is one of the most ancient historical documents that we possess. The stone was erected by King Mesha, the "*sheep-master,*" to commemorate his successful revolt when *Moab rebelled against Israel after the death of Ahab* (2 Kings i. 1).

"I made this monument to Chemosh at Korkhah," says the very interesting inscription—"a monument of Salvation, for he saved me from all invaders, and let me see my desire upon all my

---

[1] Quoted in St. Clair's *Buried Cities,* 302.

enemies. Omri was King of Israel, and he
oppressed Moab many days, for Chemosh was
angry with his land. His son followed him, and
he also said, I shall oppress Moab. In my days
Chemosh said, I will see my desire on him and
his house. And Israel surely perished for ever." [1]

Then follows a description of the taking of
cities whose inhabitants were slain "for the
pleasure of Chemosh and Moab," and torn "before
Chemosh in Kerioth," even as *Samuel hewed
Agag in pieces before Jehovah in Gilgal* (1 Sam.
xv. 33).

Later, the Israelites *rose up and smote the
Moabites*, and when Mesha *saw that the battle
was too sore for him*, he took, we read, *his eldest
son that should have reigned in his stead, and
offered him for a burnt offering upon the wall*, to
the Fire-god Molech (2 Kings iii. 27).

Molech, Milcom, or Melkarth (literally the

---

[1] *Rec.* N. S. ii. 194 *et seq.* Omri made so great an impression upon his time that we find his name often used in Assyrian
inscriptions. Samaria was known to the Assyrians as Beth-
Omri (the House or City of Omri) for centuries; and even Jehu
is called the son of Omri in the Black Obelisk inscription, about
840 B.C. In the time of Sargon Beth-Omri is superseded by
Samaria.—Rawlinson, *Hist. Ill.* 112. See *Jewish Church*, ii.
284; Renan, *Hist. d'Is.* ii. 253.

King of the City), was the abomination of the Ammonites, just as Chemosh was of the Moabites, and Ashtoreth of the Zidonians.   Probably Isaiah refers to this deity when he says of the sinful Israelitish nation, personified as an adulteress, *Thou wentest to the king with ointment* (lvii. 9), and *Tophet is ordained of old; yea, for the king it is prepared* (xxx. 33).   Molech-worship, reintroduced by Solomon in his idolatrous old age, was an evil of ancient standing in the land.   "*They sacrificed unto devils, and not to God,*" says Deuteronomy of the ungrateful people of old (xxxii. 17).   "*Yea, they sacrificed their sons and their daughters unto devils . . . unto the idols of Canaan,*" echoes the Psalmist (cvi. 37, 38).

He that *giveth any of his seed unto Molech, he shall surely be put to death,* ran the stern Mosaic law; *the people of the land shall stone him with stones* (Lev. xx.).   *And thou shalt not let any of thy seed pass through the fire to Molech . . . it is abomination . . . For in all these things the nations are defiled which I cast out before you : and the land is defiled . . . and the land itself vomiteth out her inhabitants* (xviii.).

Molech the Flame-god and Baal the Sun-god

are probably identical in worship and attributes, both being derived from the Babylonian Samas. Thus Jeremiah says of his generation, " *They built the high places of Baal, which are in the valley of the son of Hinnom, to cause their sons and their daughters to pass through the fire unto Molech ; which I commanded them not* " (xxxii. 35).[1] They are probably, too, the same as the Tyrian " Hercules," whose temple, with its pillar of shining emerald, Herodotus made a voyage to Tyre in order to see (ii. 44) ; and the Jewish traditions of their rites are confirmed by the accounts taken from other ancient authors.

"For Cronus, whom the Phoenicians call Il," says one,[2] "and who after his death was deified and instated in the planet which bears his name [*Saturn*], when king, had . . . an only son, who on that account is styled Ieoud, for so the

[1] See Kenrick, *Phoenicia*, 299, 319, 322 ; Sir G. Wilkinson in Rawlinson's *Herodotus*, ii. 81 ; 2 Kings xvii. 16, xxi. 5 ; Jer. xix. 5.

In the seventh century B.C. Josiah *defiled Topheth*, that sacrifices might no longer be held there (2 Kings xxiii. 10), and it became a place where offal and carcases were cast, and fires kept up to prevent pestilence—" *where their worm dieth not, and the fire is not quenched* " (Isaiah lxvi. 24 ; Mark ix.).

[2] Sanchoniatho, Cory's *Fragments*, p. 17. Whiston, *Josephus*, p. 675.

Phoenicians still call an only son : and when great
dangers from war beset the land he adorned the
altar, and invested this son with the emblems of
royalty, and sacrificed him."

"For among the Carthaginians," says Diodorus,
"there was a brazen statue of Saturn putting forth
the palms of his hands, bending in such a manner
towards the earth as that the boy, who was laid
upon them in order to be sacrificed, should slip off,
and so fall down headlong into a deep and fiery
furnace" (xx. 1). And Plutarch, in his treatise
De Superstitione, basing his argument against belief
in either "God or spirit" upon the immorality of
most religious rites, adds that "all the space before
the idol was filled with the din of instruments,
flutes and drums, so that the cry of lamentation
could not be heard."

All these details the learned Selden collected
in his work *De diis Syriis*; and these his contemporary Milton, touching them with the hand of
genius, shaped into the lines that have made the
gods of Canaan almost as familiar to our minds as
the gods of Greece or Rome.[1]

[1] "For the enumeration of the Syrian and Arabian deities,
it may be observed that Milton has comprised in one hundred

" First Moloch, horrid king, besmeared with blood
Of human sacrifice, and parents' tears ;
Though, for the noise of drum and timbrels loud,
Their children's cries unheard that passed through fire
To his grim idol.   Him the Ammonite
Worshipped in Rabba."

While—

       " Not content with such
Audacious neighbourhood, the wisest heart
Of Solomon he led by fraud to build
His temple right against the temple of God
On that opprobrious hill, and made his grove
The pleasant valley of Hinnom, Tophet thence
And black Gehenna called, the type of Hell.
Next Chemosh, the obscene dread of Moab's sons,

   .   .   .   .   .   .

With these came they who, from the bordering flood
Of old Euphrates to the brook that parts
Egypt from Syrian ground, had general names
Of Baalim and Ashtaroth.

   .   .   .   .   .   .

               With these in troop
Came Astoreth, whom the Phoenicians called
Astarte, queen of heaven, with crescent horns ;
To whose bright image nightly by the moon
Sidonian virgins paid their vows and songs.

---

and thirty very beautiful lines the two large and learned
syntagmas which Selden had composed on that abstruse
subject."—Gibbon, *Decline and Fall*, chap. xv. *n*. Strange that
Selden's book, the mine from which so many students have
drawn their facts and theories, should still lack a translation.
It would, I think, well repay the labours of a judicious editor.

               Thammuz came next behind,
Whose annual wound in Lebanon allured
The Syrian damsels to lament his fate
In amorous ditties all a summer's day,
While smooth Adonis from his native rock
Ran purple to the sea, supposed with blood
Of Thammuz yearly wounded."—*Paradise Lost*, I.

These were the chief Canaanitish divinities, each god worshipped with rites perhaps but slightly differing, each god probably worshipped as a "real divinity,—as supreme and absolute,— without a suspicion of those limitations which, to our mind, a plurality of gods must entail on every single god." [1]

Thus the rites imitated by Solomon were not, perhaps, so much idolatrous, as cruel, dark, impure.

And there was another form of cruelty to which the tastes of the great king inevitably led. "Les grands règnes coûtent très-cher." Under Solomon,

[1] Max Müller on the Veda—*Chips from German Workshops*, i. 27, 28. See also Kenrick, *Phoenicia*, 307: "If idolatry be defined the worship of false gods, the Phoenicians were certainly idolaters; but in the sense of image-worship, this name is less applicable to them than to the Egyptians, Assyrians, or Greeks. Their temples appear generally to have contained either no visible representation of the deity, or only rude symbols. Their religion is reprobated in the Scriptures, but rather for its cruelty than its licentiousness."

the Israelites beheld again the magnificence as of an Egyptian Pharaoh, and tasted again of the bitterness of that bondage which they had almost forgotten since the days when the Lord God redeemed them out of Egypt (Deut. xxiv. 18).

Copying the Pharaohs in their magnificence, Solomon copied them also in their disregard of human suffering. And the thousands who, under his rule, became *bearers of burdens*, and *hewers in the mountain* (2 Chron. ii. 18), must have bitterly called to mind the words which Samuel spoke to the people, when they asked to have a king *like all the nations.*

"This will be the manner of the king that shall reign over you," Samuel had told them : "He will take your sons, and appoint them for himself, for his chariots, and to be his horsemen ; and some shall run before his chariots. . . . And he will take your menservants, and your maidservants, and your goodliest young men, and your asses, and put them to his work. He will take the tenth of your sheep : and ye shall be his servants. And ye shall cry out in that day because of your king which ye shall have chosen you ; and the Lord will not hear you in that day " (1 Sam. viii. 11-18).

At first probably Solomon's *tribute of bond service* was levied only upon subject tribes—upon *all the people that were left of the Amorites, Hittites,*

Perizzites, Hivites, and Jebusites (1 Kings ix. 20),
—as had been that of David his father. For
the children of Israel were reserved the more
honourable employments, as *men of war, rulers of
chariots,* and officers over his work. But the time
came when his imperious demands could only be
satisfied by the raising of a *levy out of all Israel*
(1 Kings v. 13) ; and it is a significant fact, says
Stanley, that the word Nitssab, "which elsewhere
is used for the garrisons planted in a hostile
country, is now employed for officers appointed by
the king of Israel over his own subjects." [1]

Moreover, the exactions of Solomon tended not
only to breed discontent throughout the people,
but to *break the brotherhood between Judah and
Israel* (Zech. xi. 14). For the rural tribes of the
north, Ephraim and Manasseh, took no pride in
the glories of the House of Judah. To them—to
the "House of Joseph"—had in earlier days
belonged all the rulers of the land ; and already
we see the tribal jealousy appearing when, after
Absalom's revolt against David, *all the people of
Judah,* and *half* only of the people of Israel,
conducted the king to take his own again.

---

[1] *Jewish Church,* ii. 192.

"And, behold, all the men of Israel came to the king, and said unto the king, Why have our brethren the men of Judah stolen thee away ? . . . And all the men of Judah answered the men of Israel, Because the king is near of kin to us. . . . And the words of the men of Judah were fiercer than the words of the men of Israel" (2 Sam. xix. 41-43).

Bitterly the men of Israel now resented the exactions of the new régime; and in appointing the young Ephrathite, Jeroboam, to be *ruler over all the charge of the house of Joseph*, Solomon had, nothing doubting, given a chief to the revolt. One rising there had been, even during the great king's lifetime, but it had been quelled, and Jeroboam had fled away into Egypt, where a new dynasty, unfriendly to the house of Judah, had lately usurped the throne of the priest-kings, Solomon's allies.

In Egypt Jeroboam bided his time, and when Solomon rested with his fathers, and of his seed left behind him Rehoboam, "even the foolishness of the people, and one that had no understanding" (Ecclus. xlvii. 23), then, when the smouldering discontent was ready to burst into flame, the Ephrathite returned to his native land.

To elect the new king the deputies " assembled,

not in Jerusalem or Hebron, but in Shechem, the ancient capital of Joseph,—a significant hint." [1]

" And Rehoboam went to Shechem : for all Israel were come to Shechem to make him king. And it came to pass, when Jeroboam the son of Nebat, who was yet in Egypt, heard of it (for he was fled from the presence of king Solomon, and Jeroboam dwelt in Egypt), that they sent and called him. And Jeroboam and all the congregation of Israel came, and spake unto Rehoboam, saying, Thy father made our yoke grievous ; now therefore make thou the grievous service of thy father, and his heavy yoke which he put upon us, lighter, and we will serve thee. . . .

"And the king answered the people roughly, and forsook the old men's counsel that they gave him; and spake to them after the counsel of the young men, saying, My father made your yoke heavy, and I will add to your yoke : my father also chastised you with whips, but I will chastise you with scorpions " (1 Kings xii. 1-14).

" *To your tents, O Israel : see to thine own house, David,*" was again the cry ; *there was none that followed the house of David, but the tribe of Judah only.*

Thus did the Hebrew Empire fall apart, after lasting less than a century. And finally, the work of David and Solomon was shattered by the Pharaoh of Egypt in one campaign, when, in the

[1] Ewald, *Hist.* iii. 312.

fifth year of Rehoboam, the children of Israel for
the first time met the Egyptians in war.

Sheshank, or *Shishak king of Egypt*—he is the
first Pharaoh mentioned by name in the Bible—
came up against Jerusalem, we read ; *and he took
away the treasures of the house of the Lord, and
the treasures of the king's house ; he even took away
all : and he took away all the shields of gold which
Solomon had made* (1 Kings xiv. 25, 26).

Shishak's own account of the matter was
sculptured on the outer wall of the great temple
at Karnak, where it still remains for all to see
—the only direct allusion to Israelitish history
on the Egyptian monuments.   Here the Pharaoh
"is represented as striking down the conquered
Hebrews with a colossal club, while beside him
run long rows of embattled shields, within each of
which is the name of a vanquished city."[1]

Very different were the destinies of the two
kingdoms into which Solomon's empire was divided
after his death.   In Judah, the house of David
maintained its hold against intrigues within and

---

[1] Sayce, *Fresh Light*, 118. See also Stanley, *Jewish Church*,
ii. 384 ; Brugsch, *Egypt*, 375, new ed.

confederations from without her borders;[1] and
when Amon crowned the wicked deeds of his
father Manasseh, so that *his servants conspired
against him, and slew the king in his own house,
the people of the land,* we read, punished the con-
spirators and set Josiah upon his father's throne.
The kings who were taken captive from Jerusalem
to Babylon, four hundred years after the disruption,
were *kings of the house of David.*

But "the kingdom of Israel had been founded
by usurpation, and its history is that of a line of
usurpers."[2]   When Jezebel threw out at Jehu
that ringing taunt, "*Had Zimri peace, who slew
his master?*" she put into a sentence the history
of the kingly houses of Samaria.

In poetry, in literature, the north was always
far in advance of the sister kingdom.   But *in
Judah is God known . . . In Salem is his taber-
nacle, and his dwelling in Zion* (Psalm lxxvi.
1, 2).   *The Lord loveth the gates of Zion more than
all the dwellings of Jacob* (Psalm lxxxvii. 2).

[1] 2 Kings xxi. 19, and xvi. 5.   In relation to the latter,
Isaiah (viii. 6) denounces those in Jerusalem "*that go softly,
and rejoice in Rezin and Remaliah's son.*"   See page 171.

[2] Sayce, *Isaiah,* 68.   See also Renan, *Hist.* ii. 244 ; Stanley,
Jewish Church, ii. 381.

In Judah there was unity of religious worship ; while in Samaria there were *high places in all their cities*. Jeroboam, "doubling the sin" of Aaron, *took counsel, and made two calves of gold, and said unto the people, It is too much for you to go up to Jerusalem : behold thy gods, O Israel, which brought thee up out of the land of Egypt. And he set the one in Bethel, and the other put he in Dan. And this thing became a sin* (1 Kings xii. 28-30).

It is supposed that, in the fourth century after the disruption, an "elohist" compiler of Jerusalem, taking as his basis the northern or Jehovist annals, compiled the two Books of Kings, and was able to impress upon his work the mark of that unity of faith which kept the Jewish creed upstanding in spite of all the reverses of the Jewish people. The *high places in all their cities*, the *images and groves in every high hill*, the *calves of gold* in Bethel and in Dan, these formed the sin of Jeroboam the son of Nebat, wherewith he made Israel to sin. "*Therefore*," said Judah, "*the Lord was very angry with Israel*" (2 Kings xvii. 9, 10, 18).

"Le Décalogue," says Renan, "est la loi de Moïse telle qu'on la résumait à Jérusalem. . . . Dans le Décalogue, en effet, est achevé le retour d'Israel au culte pur, à ce monothéisme qu'on entrevoit aux origines de la vie patriarcale et dont le peuple avait devié en adoptant un dieu national. Iahvé et Élohim ne font plus qu'un. Iahvé n'est plus seulement le dieu d'Israel; il est le dieu du ciel, de la terre, du genre humain. . . . Ce funeste nom de Iahvé, [on] à fini par le supprimer en le déclarant imprononçable." [1]

And thus it came to pass that the Hebrews, if a "destroyed nation," have been "an indestructible people. Without the commercial or colonising energy of their Phoenician kinsmen, without the architectural genius and patient industry which built the monuments and cities of Egypt, without the ambition and courage which raised their Assyrian brethren to empire and a sovereign civilisation, without the poetic and speculative genius of the Greeks, without the martial and political capacity of the Romans, the politically unimportant and despised Hebrews have excelled these gifted nations, singly and combined, in religious faculty, and in the power exercised through religion on mankind." [2]

---

[1] Renan, *Hist.* ii. 398, 406
[2] Fairbairn, *Phil. of Religion and History*, 308.

NOTE.—The covenant name of the God of Israel occurs on the Moabite stone, in the latter half of the ninth century B.C., written exactly as in the Old Testament— a proof, if any were needed, that the feeling which later prevented the Jews from pronouncing it had not then taken shape. But the name has descended to us in a very incorrect form; for the Hebrew alphabet represented consonants only, and not vowels, and when Hebrew ceased to be a living language the pronunciation of the words became a matter of tradition. To avoid the danger of its being altogether forgotten, the Masoretes or Scribes, in the sixth century A.D., "invented a system of symbols which should represent the pronunciation of the Hebrew of the Old Testament"; and it is in accordance with this system that Hebrew is now taught. But there was one word which these Masoretes dared not utter. For the name of the God of Israel they directed that the word Adonai (Lord) should be read, and this they indicated by writing under the consonants Y H V H the vowels of Adonai, a or e, o, a, thus—$Y_a H_o V_a H$. The scholars who first revived the study of Hebrew in modern Europe, misunderstanding this, read the word as "Yehovah," which, passing from German into English, became our Jehovah.—Sayce, *Fresh Light*, 74; P. J. Smyth, *Old Documents and New Bible*, 98; Clodd, *Jewish History*, 189.

CHAPTER IV

*"Behold, the Assyrian was a cedar in Lebanon with fair branches, and with a shadowing shroud, and of an high stature; and his top was among the thick boughs. The waters made him great, the deep set him up on high with her rivers running round about his plants, and sent out her little rivers unto all the trees of the field. Therefore his height was exalted above all the trees of the field . . . and under his shadow dwelt all great nations. Thus was he fair in his greatness, in the length of his branches for his root was by great waters. . . . I made the nations to shake at the sound of his fall, when I cast him down to hell with them that descend into the pit."—*Ezek. xxxi. 3-16.

*"Woe to the bloody city! It is all full of lies and robbery; the prey departeth not; the noise of a whip, and the noise of the rattling of the wheels, and of the prancing horses, and of the jumping chariots . . . . Behold, I am against thee, saith the Lord of hosts."—*Nahum iii. 1-5. *"I will make thy grave; for thou art vile."—*Nahum i. 14.

WE have seen that, after the days of the great founder of the Assyrian Empire, Tiglath-Pileser I., Assyrian history becomes for a while obscure. In 885 B.C. a great revival took place, when Assur-nazir-pal, one of the most ferocious and most energetic of her kings, coming to the throne of Assyria, carried her arms far and wide through Western Asia.

"The countries, all of them, from the rising of the sun to the setting of the sun, he has made to submit to his feet," says his inscription:[1] every-

KING ASSUR-NAZIR-PAL WALKING IN A MOUNTAINOUS COUNTRY.
After Rawlinson (Murray).

where his steps seem to have been marked by victories, and by the wreaking of a terrible vengeance upon his foes. "I cut off their noses, ears, and fingers; the eyes of the soldiers I put out"; "With their blood I dyed the mountain"; "I built a pyramid with the heads of the dead; the living soldiers I impaled on stakes round about

---

[1] *Guide to Nimroud Central Saloon in British Museum,* 19. See also *Rec.* N. S. ii.

their city," are phrases which constantly recur in the ghastly annals of his reign.

In the time of Assur-nazir-pal's son and successor, Shalmaneser II. (860-825 B.C.), occurred the first contact of Assyria with the Israelitish monarchies. Hadadeser[1] of Damascus, the second Benhadad whose wars with Israel fill so large a space in the Books of Kings, attempting to stem the torrent of Assyrian invasion, had formed a league with the Hittites of Hamath against it; and "Akhabbu (Ahab) of the country of the Israelites" is mentioned in an inscription,[2] as forming one of the confederacy; which must in that case have occurred during those *three years without war between Syria and Israel* mentioned in 1 Kings xxii. 1.

Many years later, when the confederacy had been shattered at Karkar, when Ahab had again broken with Benhadad and had lost his life in trying to recover Ramoth-gilead, when Moab had

[1] The name on the monuments is Addu-'idri (=Hadadhidri). See *Rec.* N. S. iv. 100.

[2] Upon a monolith from Kurkh, which, with the celebrated Black Obelisk found at Kouyunjik (Nineveh) and the bronze gates of a temple, contain the chief annals and inscriptions of Shalmaneser II. All are now in the British Museum.—*Rec.* N. S. iv. 36. For descriptions see *Guide to Nimroud Central Saloon*, 26-45; Sayce, *Assyria*, 146-148.

rebelled against Israel, and when Hazael reigned
at Damascus in the stead of his murdered master,
Shalmaneser seemed to have again marched to the
West and to have received the first Israelitish
tribute (841 B.C.).

"In my eighteenth year, for the sixteenth time
I crossed the Euphrates," says the inscription on
the Black Obelisk; "Hazael, of Damascus, trusted
in the might of his army, and assembled his army
without number . . . I fought with him; I overthrew him. . . . In Damascus, his royal city, I
shut him up. . . . At that time I received the
tribute of the Tyrians, of the Sidonians, and of
Jehu, son of Omri." We see in bas-relief the
Israelitish ambassador, kneeling before the king,
his face bowed to the ground. He is dressed in
a long simple robe, with a sort of Phrygian cap.
His beard is short, and his hair falls to his
shoulders. Behind him come the tribute-
bearers,[1] and over all is the king's inscription—
"The tribute of Yaua (Jehu) son of Humri

[1] "In drawing one of these familiar faces from the monument," says a writer quoted in St. Clair's *Buried Cities* (348),
"I was ready to believe that it belonged to a lineal ancestor
of the London 'Clo'men.' The bag falling down the stooping
back deepened this impression."

(Omri) : silver and gold, a golden cup, golden
vases, golden vessels, golden buckets, lead, a
staff for the hand of the king, and sceptres, I
received."

But no record of this tribute is found in the
Bible ; and perhaps we must not take too literally
the high-sounding inscriptions upon the official
stelae of Assyria and Egypt, just as we must not
assume, upon the faith of Chinese proclamations
of to-day, that the whole world is tributary to the
Emperor of China.[1]

Certain it is that for nearly a hundred years after
the great victories of Shalmaneser II. (whose last
personal campaign was in 834 B.C.), Assyria was a
prey to internal dissensions ; and although in 804
another prince of Shalmaneser's dynasty had besieged and taken Damascus, this did but afford to
Jeroboam II. the opportunity to *restore the coast of
Israel from the entering of Hamath unto the sea of
the plain* (2 Kings xiv. 25).

For nearly a hundred years no Assyrian army
came to disturb the petty politics of Palestine; and
in the days of the houses of Omri and of Jehu, Syria
(the other kingdom carved out of the dominions of

[1] Renan, *Hist. d'Is.* ii. 406.

Solomon) was evidently the most dreaded adversary of Israel. Campaign after campaign was formed for retaking Ramoth-gilead, the great frontier fortress. *"Know ye that Ramoth-gilead is ours, and we be still, and take it not out of the hand of the king of Syria?"* was the standing appeal of the kings of Israel to their servants. *"Shall I go up against Ramoth-gilead, or shall I forbear?"* was the standing question in Israelitish politics.[1]

The earlier prophets (Amos, Obadiah,[2] Joel) make no mention of Assyria. To them *it is an evil time* (Amos v. 13), because Jeroboam has revived the luxury and license of the court of Ahab; because the poor are oppressed, and the rich are selfishly indulgent. In Amos, the shepherd of Tekoa, whose writings bring the peasant life of his day so freshly and vividly

---

[1] 1 Kings xxii. 3, 6, 15, etc. See Stanley, *Jewish Church*, ii. 344.

[2] There is much difference of opinion as to the date of Obadiah. Stanley (*Jewish Church*, ii. 556) makes him after fall of Jerusalem; Pusey before. Renan (ii. 445) thinks that he belonged to the time of Jeroboam II. "L'horizon politique est, en pareil cas, le véritable *criterium* pour juger de l'âge des morceaux." "Rien de plus facile que de classer les prophètes en antérieurs ou postérieurs à l'entrée en scène des Assyriens" (ii. 297).

before us, Renan recognises "la première voix de tribun que le monde ait entendue." "Nous croyons que les plus anciens avocats de l'opprimé furent les prophètes d'Israel," he says (ii. 425 ; i. 227).

"*Hear this word, ye kine of Bashan, that are in the mountain of Samaria, which oppress the poor, which crush the needy*," cries Amos (iv. 1).   "*Woe to them that are at ease in Zion . . . that lie upon beds of ivory, and stretch themselves upon their couches, and eat the lambs out of the flock, and the calves out of the midst of the stall . . . but they are not grieved for the affliction of Joseph*" (vi. 1-6).

The enemies of Israel are those of her own house, *because they sold the righteous for silver, and the poor for a pair of shoes* (Amos ii. 6); Syria, and hated Edom *because he did pursue his brother with the sword, and did cast off all pity* (i. 11) ; Tyre in her wanton luxury ; Ashdod and *Ekron of the Philistines.*   Of a *captivity beyond Damascus* there is no serious question.

All at once the scene changes.   In 745 [1]—the

---

[1] Accurate Assyrian chronology dates from about 900 B.C.— *i.e.* just before the time of Assur-nazir-pal. The Assyrian canon, discovered by Sir H. Rawlinson in 1862, then begins its record, which contains a full list of the yearly eponyms, or officers after whom each year was called—every event being stated to

M

exact date is now known from the cuneiform tablets—the throne of Assyria was seized by a military adventurer called Pulu, or Pul: and a new order of things began.

Taking the name of Tiglath-Pileser (III.) after his renowned predecessor, the first of the name, Pul set about founding an empire in Western Asia, such as the world had never seen before. Assyria became the first example of a great central-ised bureaucracy, the first example of a military despotism, a grinding oppression in which no moral or religious consideration could find a place.

The Pharaohs had been as wealthy, and in many ways as warlike, as the monarchs of Assyria; but the Egyptian character was not less different from the Assyrian than were the lightness, the elegance, the perfection in which the Pharaohs delighted, from the massive richness which found favour in Assyria. We see the difference in the physique of the two peoples—nay, their very dress

have occurred "in the eponymy" of such an one. The chron-ology of Assyria, and therefore of much of the Old Testament, has been accurately fixed by means of this document.—Sayce, *Assyria*, 102 ; Smith, *Assyria*, 40 ; Budge, *Babylonian Life and Hist.*, 34.

declares it. For the simple linen garments of the Pharaohs are so light, so marvellously fine, that they scarcely hide the limbs they cover; while the Assyrian kings always appear upon the monuments loaded with heavy, stiff materials, shaggy, and over-weighted with gold and silver, with fringes and embroideries.[1]

Robust, broad-shouldered, and large-limbed, with a vigour of mind and body which no other Semitic race has ever equalled or approached, these "Romans of Asia" ruthlessly fought their way to absolute dominion. Like the Romans they "had a genius for organising and administering, for making and obeying laws, and for submitting to the restraints of an inexorable discipline."[2] Their army formed the first example of a mercenary soldiery, *hired among the nations, learning war* as a profession.[3] It was the best organised war machine the world had ever seen, the best drilled, and above all the best equipped; and to it the Assyrians trusted to do

[1] Maspéro, *Ancient Egypt and Assyria*, 272.

[2] Sayce, *Races of Old Testament*, 137. See also Smith, *Assyria*, 14; Renan, ii. 457; Maspéro, *Ancient Egypt and Assyria*, 320, 364.

[3] Hosea viii. 10; Isaiah ii. 4; Micah iv. 3.

for them what industry and trade had done for their neighbours in the West.

They came down upon their enemies like a whirlwind. *Clothed with blue, captains and rulers, all of them desirable young men, horsemen riding upon horses* (Ezek. xxiii. 6), they swept through the plains of Syria. *They shall come with speed swiftly : none shall be weary nor stumble among them ; none shall slumber nor sleep ; . . . whose arrows are sharp, and all their bows bent, their horses' hoofs shall be counted like flint, and their wheels like a whirlwind : their roaring shall be like a lion, they shall roar like young lions : yea, they shall roar, and lay hold of the prey, and shall carry it away safe, and none shall deliver it,* said the prophet (Is. v. 26-29).

Caring for nothing save warfare and plunder, their literature and art, like their religion, were borrowed from Babylonia. The language of their learned men was the ancient Accadian tongue, of the land whence Asshur *went forth and builded Nineveh* (Gen. x. 11); nearly every tablet in their library was plundered from the libraries of Babylonia : in a land of stone, they built their houses of brick, and raised their palace-temples high on artificial platforms, like those which were essential in the alluvial plains below. Their gods were the ancient gods of Babylonia, to whom they added only goddesses—pale reflections of the Accadian gods—and among whom they gave greater prominence to Samas the sun. For Istar had been the sole goddess of the Accadians, and Samas was but one of their lesser divinities ; whereas the Semites of Assyria and Babylonia were sunworshippers, and Samas was to them Bel or Baal, the Lord.[1]

They adopted the rubric of Babylonia, and among their tablets are many containing psalms and incantations.

"Seven are they ! seven are they !"

says the hymn of evil spirits.

"In the abyss of the deep, seven are they,
  In the brightness of Heaven, seven are they.
  In the abyss of the deep in a place was their growth.
  Male they are not, female they are not.
  Moreover the deep is their pathway.
  Wife they have not, child is not born to them.
  Law and order they know not.
  Prayer and supplication hear they not.
  Among the thorns of the mountain was their growth."

---

[1] Sayce, *Assyria*, 56.

"For the tearful supplication of the heart, let the glorious name of every god be invoked sixty-five times, and then the heart shall have peace,"[1] says the rubric.

But in truth the Assyrians were not, like the early Babylonians, a religious-minded people. "It is significant that, whereas in Babylonia we find the remains of scarcely any great buildings except temples, the great buildings of Assyria were the royal palaces."[2]

And perhaps that which most shocked the Hebrews in the religion of their conquerors was its arrogant impiety. "*Wherefore*," said the prophet, "*it shall come to pass, that when the Lord hath performed his whole work upon mount Zion and on Jerusalem, I will punish the fruit of the stout heart of the king of Assyria, and the glory of his high looks. For he saith, By the strength of my hand I have done it, and by my wisdom ; . . . I have removed the bounds of the people . . . and I have put down the inhabitants.*"[3]

---

[1] Budge, *Babylonian Life and History*, 138 ; Sayce, *Assyria*, 73.

[2] Sayce, *Assyria*, 67 ; Renan, ii. 457.

[3] Isaiah x. 12 ; also xxxvii. 24, etc.

There is no mistaking the effect which these
sombre and arrogant conquerors, with their alien
civilisation and their strange-sounding names,
produced upon the prophets of Israel. For a
prophet, a seer, is one who sees, *the man whose
eyes are open* (Numb. xxiv. 15). "To see clearly,"
says Ruskin, " is poetry, prophecy, and religion,—
all in one." And the seers of Israel were not slow
to recognise that this new Assyrian empire was
to change the face of the world.

Hosea, the Jeremiah of Israel ; Isaiah, "great
and faithful in his vision" (Ecclus. xlviii. 22) ;
Micah, the Morasthite, are not behind their fore-
runners in hate of oppression and wrong-doing.
More bitterly even than Amos and Joel did
they denounce the wickedness and corruption of
their day—the social system under which, in the
presence of overwhelming danger, Zion was built
with blood, and Jerusalem with iniquity.

In burning words Micah denounces the oppression of the poor by the rich (iii. 1-4), the social
system wherein *the heads thereof judge for reward, and the priests thereof teach for hire, and
the prophets thereof divine for money* (ver. 11).
The good man is perished out of the earth: and

there is none upright among men: they all lie in wait for blood; they hunt every man his brother with a net. That they may do evil with both hands earnestly, the prince asketh, and the judge asketh for a reward (vii. 2, 3).

"Hear the word of the Lord, ye children of Israel: for the Lord hath a controversy with the inhabitants of the land, because there is no truth, nor mercy, nor knowledge of God in the land," said Hosea (iv. 1).

"Woe unto them," cried Isaiah, "that join house to house, that lay field to field, till there be no place, that they may be placed alone in the midst of the earth! . . . Woe unto them that rise up early in the morning, that they may follow strong drink; that continue until night, till wine inflame them! . . . Woe unto them that draw iniquity with cords of vanity, and sin as it were with a cart rope. . . . Woe unto them that call evil good, and good evil; that put darkness for light, and light for darkness; that put bitter for sweet, and sweet for bitter! . . . Woe unto them that are mighty to drink wine, and men of strength to mingle strong drink: which justify the wicked for reward, and take away the righteousness of the righteous from him!" (v. 8-23).

"Because the daughters of Zion are haughty, and walk with stretched forth necks and wanton eyes, walking and mincing as they go, and making a tinkling with their feet. . . . The Lord will take away the bravery of their tinkling ornaments about their feet . . . the chains, and the bracelets, and the mufflers . . . the rings, and nose jewels, the changeable suits of apparel, and the mantles and the wimples, and the crisping pins" (iii. 16-22).

"What mean ye that ye beat my people to pieces, and grind the faces of the poor ? saith the Lord God of hosts" (iii. 15).

The great distinction between Isaiah and the prophets who went before him lies in his knowledge of the instrument by which God will chastise His people. The Assyrian, he sees, is to be the rod of the Lord's anger, and the staff in his hand is to be the Lord's indignation. *I will send him against an hypocritical nation, and against the people of my wrath will I give him a charge, to take the spoil, and to take the prey, and to tread them down like the mire of the streets* (Is. x. 6).

The Millennium of Isaiah is a time, not only when the wolf *shall dwell with the lamb,* and when *Ephraim shall not envy Judah, and Judah shall not vex Ephraim;* but when Israel shall be *the third with Egypt and with Assyria . . . whom the Lord of hosts shall bless, saying, Blessed be Egypt my people, and Assyria the work of my hands* (xix. 24, 25).

Every page of the book of Isaiah carries us back to the struggle which for almost fifty years he waged against the ignorance, the self-indulgence, the wrong - headedness of his day.

"La pensée et la langue arrivent chez lui," says a master of style, "à ce degré de parfait embrassement au delà duquel on sent ou que la langue sera brisée ou que la pensée sera gênée. . . . Pas une page dans son recueil qui n'ait été de circonstance, qui ne porte le cachet du jour, qui ne soit l'écho éloquent d'une situation donnée, vue à travers le verre coloré d'une forte et unique passion." [1]

Babylonia was the first to feel the effects of the new state of things at Nineveh. But soon Tiglath-Pileser turned his arms against the Syrian kings, and among those who were forced to offer him tribute, we read upon his monuments the names of Menihimme (Menahem) of Samaria, Rezin of Damascus, and Hiram of Tyre.

And Pul the king of Assyria came against the land ; and Menahem gave Pul a thousand talents of silver, that his hand might be with him to confirm the kingdom in his hand. And Menahem exacted the money of Israel, even of all the mighty men of wealth, of each man fifty shekels of silver, to give to the king of Assyria. So the king of Assyria

[1] Renan, *Hist. du Peuple d'Israel*, ii. 480, 481.

turned back, and stayed not there in the land (2 Kings xv. 19).   This was about 738 B.C.

Four years later,[1] when one of those palace conspiracies so common in Israel had placed Pekah the son of Remaliah upon the throne of Samaria, a decisive step was taken in the politics of the Syrian kingdoms.

"*And it came to pass in the days of Ahaz . . . king of Judah, that Rezin the king of Syria, and Pekah the son of Remaliah, king of Israel, went up toward Jerusalem to war against it. . . . And it was told the house of David, saying, Syria is confederate with Ephraim: and his heart was moved, and the heart of his people, as the trees of the wood are moved with the wind.   Then said the Lord unto Isaiah, Go forth now to meet Ahaz . . . and say unto him, Take heed, and be quiet ; fear not, neither be faint-hearted*" (Isaiah vii. 1-4).[2]

---

[1] 2 Kings xvi. 1 would imply an interval of at least twenty years between the tribute of Menahem to "Pul" and the tribute of Ahaz to Tiglath-Pileser.   But if Prof. Sayce is right in considering Tiglath-Pileser and Pul to be one and the same, the Assyrian canon must correct the Scripture record, which (be it remembered) has passed through the hands of many generations of copyists.

[2] The king and the prophet met *at the end of the conduit of the upper pool in the highway of the fuller's field,* where no doubt

Thus for the first time did Isaiah preach, and (as so often later) preach in vain, his doctrine of *quietness and confidence.* " *Take heed, and be quiet; fear not, neither be faint-hearted,*" he said.

But Ahaz, in his panic at the lesser evil, precipitated a greater. He *sent messengers to Tiglath-Pileser king of Assyria, saying, I am thy servant and thy son : come up, and save me out of the hand of the king of Syria, and out of the hand of the king of Israel, which rise up against me. And Ahaz took the silver and gold that was found in the house of the Lord, and in the treasures of the king's house, and sent it for a present to the king of Assyria. And the king of Assyria hearkened unto him* (2 Kings xvi. 7).

No doubt Tiglath-Pileser was ready enough to

Ahaz was visiting the *waters of Shiloah that go softly,* with a view to the water supply of Jerusalem during the siege. In the Pool of Siloam, ten years ago, the priceless inscription was discovered which shows us the form of Hebrew writing used before the exile. It tells how the tunnel was made, the excavators working from opposite ends till they "struck pick against pick, one against another" (*Rec.* N. S. i. 173). There is unfortunately no indication of date. Renan thinks that at the time of the visit of Ahaz the tunnel may have actually been in course of construction, and this would place the inscription "bien près de l'an 740 " (ii. 509). But Sayce (*Fresh Light,* 104) seems inclined to place it as far back as the reign of Solomon.

do so. He had never yet pushed his conquests beyond Samaria, and now the submission of the king of Judah (whose father had been the ally of Hamath, Assyria's most powerful enemy) left him master as far as the borders of Egypt. Rezin was utterly defeated, besieged in his capital and slain; the cities of the Philistines were taken; Tyre was fined; Edom subdued; the Israelitish tribes beyond the Jordan carried into captivity.

" The towns of Gilead and Abel (beth-Maachah) in the province of Beth-Omri, the widespread (district of Napta)li to its whole extent I turned into the territory of Assyria," [1] says the inscription. "The land of Beth-Omri I overran. Some of its inhabitants (with their goods) I transported to Assyria. Pekah their king I put to death, and I appointed Hoshea to the sovereignty over them. Ten (talents of gold . . . talents of silver as) their tribute I received, and I transported them to Assyria."

In Damascus, the conquered capital of Syria,

---

[1] Sayce, *Assyria*, 150. The words are almost the echo of the Book of Kings: he *took Ijon, and Abel-beth-maachah, and Janoah, and Kedesh, and Hazor, and Gilead, and Galilee, all the land of Naphtali, and carried them captive to Assyria* (2 Kings xv. 29).

Tiglath-Pileser held a court; and there King Ahaz went to meet him (2 Kings xvi. 10) and to do him homage. From that visit Ahaz brought back not only *the fashion* of the Sun-god's *altar and the pattern of it*, but also many other relics of the Syrian Baal-worship. We read how he *made his son to pass through the fire, according to the abominations of the heathen;* of his *sun-dial*, and later, of the *horses that the kings of Judah had given to the sun*.[1]

And in the time of his distress did he trespass yet more against the Lord: this is that king Ahaz. For he sacrificed unto the gods of Damascus, which smote him: and he said, Because the gods of the kings of Syria help them, therefore will I sacrifice to them, that they may help me. But they were the ruin of him, and of all Israel (2 Chron. xxviii. 22). "The price paid for the Assyrian aid was much more than the treasures of the temple and his palace; it was the independence and honour of the realm itself." [2] For *Tiglath-Pileser king of*

---

[1] 2 Kings xvi. 3, xxiii. 11; Is. xxxviii. 8.

Ahaz is called Jehoahaz upon the cuneiform tablets, but the Bible writers evidently would not use Jehovah's name in connection with this detested king; *for the Lord brought Judah low because of Ahaz* (2 Chron. xxviii. 19).

[2] Ewald, *Hist.* iv. 171.

Assyria came unto him, and distressed him, but strengthened him not.

From that time forward the heavy sword of Assyria was cast into the scale of Palestinian politics. From that time forward the two great empires of the ancient world, Egypt and Assyria, stood practically face to face. Midway between them lay the little kingdoms of Syria. The road from the Nile valley to the Euphrates lay through the plain of Philistia, and along the narrow strip to the north, where the Phoenician cities *were situate at the entry of the sea.* By that way the armies of Egypt and Assyria had to pass whenever there was war between the two great rivals. Palestine "was on the high road from one to the other of these mighty powers, the prize for which they contended, the battlefield on which they fought, the lofty bridge over which they ascended and descended respectively into the deep basins of the Nile and Euphrates." [1]

Small as was her territory, she was an ally well worth a struggle. For when the children of Israel "prepared for war," they could " keep the passages of the hill country," by which "it was

[1] Stanley, *Sinai and Palestine*, 116.

easy to stop them that would come up." They
could "shut up the passages," and fortify all the
tops of the high hills, and lay "impediments in
the champaign countries" (Judith iv. v.). And so
it came to pass that they were forced to take one
side or the other in the great struggle between
their powerful neighbours ; and to suffer the
vengeance of the victor if they had sided with the
vanquished.

No wonder, then, that the little kingdoms of
Israel and Judah were distracted by plans of rival
alliances.   Isaiah is full of references to the
subject. 'It pervades Hosea from end to end; and
he is the first to take up the cry against them.
"*Ephraim also is like a silly dove without heart :
they call to Egypt, they go to Assyria,*" he says
(vii. 11). "*They do make a covenant with the
Assyrians, and oil is carried into Egypt*" (xii. 1).

Egypt was the nearest at hand, and there
lingered yet in the minds of men memories of the
time when she had been mistress, not only of
Syria, but of all the country between the Euphrates
and the Nile. Since then, however, she had
declined in power, and the new Ethiopian dynasty
which had seized the throne was too much

occupied in establishing itself to be an useful or
a powerful ally. It was useless, then, to trust in
the shadow of Egypt, and urgently did Isaiah
denounce the great party in Jerusalem who tried
to strengthen themselves in the strength of Pharaoh.
"Therefore shall the strength of Pharaoh be your
shame," he said, *"and the trust in the shadow of*
Egypt your confusion" (xxx. 3).

In 727 Tiglath-Pileser III. died, and his crown
was seized by one of his generals, afterwards
called Shalmaneser V., a king of whom we know
little, except that under him began the long and
memorable siege of Samaria, with which ended
the kingdom of Israel.

The moment of a revolution in Assyria no
doubt seemed to Hoshea, the Israelitish king,
favourable for revolting against his suzerain. In
spite of the warnings of the prophets he turned
for help to *So, king of Egypt.* This So, or Sabako,
was a descendant of the old Ramesside kings of
the xxth dynasty, who, driven from power in
Egypt, had taken refuge in Ethiopia. He had
marched northward, re-conquered Lower Egypt,
and founded the xxvth (Ethiopian) dynasty;
but, though he accepted the presents of Hoshea

and gave him promises of support, he was too much occupied in consolidating his own power to help any foreign state.

" *Woe to the crown of pride, to the drunkards of Ephraim,*" cried Isaiah, "*whose glorious beauty is a fading flower ! . . . Behold, the Lord hath a mighty and strong one, which as a tempest of hail and a destroying storm, as a flood of mighty waters over-flowing, shall cast down to the earth with the hand*" (xxviii. 1-3).   But the people would not hearken. Isaiah's insistence upon the great truths which it was his mission to unfold seemed to them but vain and wearisome repetition.   *The word of the Lord was unto them precept upon precept, precept upon precept; line upon line, line upon line; here a little, and there a little*—" *tsav la-tsav, tsav la-tsav—kav la-kav, kav la-kav—ze'ĕr sham, ze'ĕr sham.*" To Isaiah it seemed that in their blindness they said, "*We have made a covenant with death, and with hell are we at agreement*" (xxviii. 13, 15).

Soon *the king of Assyria found conspiracy in Hoshea: for he had sent messengers to So king of Egypt, and brought no present to the king of Assyria, as he had done year by year: therefore the king of Assyria shut him up, and bound him in prison. Then the king of Assyria came up throughout all the land, and went up to Samaria, and besieged it three years* (2 Kings xvii. 4, xviii. 9).

Assyrian sieges were long: they *cast banks* about a doomed city, sat down before it, and waited. "*I will camp against thee round about, and will lay siege against thee with a mount, and I will raise forts against thee*," they said (Is. xxix. 3).

Tyre was closely invested also, and Josephus preserves for us a fragment of Menander, describing the sufferings of its inhabitants. "And this is what is written in the Syrian archives concerning Shalmaneser the king of Assyria," he says (ix. 14, 2).

The extremity of Tyre was watched with exultation by her enemies in Israel. Like the Puritans and Covenanters of Scottish history, the prophets felt a bitter resentment against the centres of luxury and commerce, which (as they thought) had corrupted the whole world round; and they sympathised rather with the common enemy than with their fellow-victims. In the midst of their own perils they inveigh against

Tyre, and exultingly proclaim that the *Lord hath
given a commandment against the merchant city;
the Lord of hosts hath purposed it, to stain the
pride of all glory* (Isaiah xxiii. 9, 11).[1]

But before either siege could be brought to an
end Shalmaneser died (722 B.C.), and the crown
was seized by another usurper who called himself
Sargon, after the Sargon of Accad who ruled in
Babylonia in the earliest ages of her history.

Sargon made short work of the siege of

---

[1] The expression *her own feet shall carry her afar off to
sojourn* may (thinks Renan) refer to the colonisation of
Carthage—Cartha yena, the New City (*Hist. d'Is.* ii. 526).
According to Josephus, Menander the Ephesian gave a complete
list of the Tyrian kings from Hiram to the building of Carthage.
'Ithobalus, priest of Astarte, the father of Jezebel, assumed the
throne about fifty years after Hiram's death; he reigned thirty-
two years; he was succeeded by his son Badezorus who reigned
six years; he was succeeded by Metgenus his son; he reigned
nine years; Pygmalion succeeded him; he reigned forty-seven
years. Now in the seventh year of his reign his sister fled
away from him, and built the city of Carthage in Libya.' So the
whole time from the reign of Hiram till the building of Carthage
amounts to the sum of 155 years and 8 months" (Cont. Ap.
i. 18).

The name Dido belongs to the same Semitic root as David,
"Beloved"; while the Carthaginian Hasdrubal was the man
whose "help Baal is"; and Hamilcar the man whom "Milcar
graciously granted" (*Dict. of Bible*, art. "Phoenicians"). See
page 140.

Samaria. "In the beginning of my reign the city of Samaria I besieged, I captured," he says; "27,280 of its inhabitants I carried away; fifty chariots in the midst of them I collected, and the rest of their goods I seized; I set my governor over them and laid upon them the tribute of the former king (Hoshea)."[1]   Then, as once again, in Ramah was there a voice heard, *lamentation and bitter weeping; Rachel,* the mother of Joseph, *weeping for her children refused to be comforted, because they were not* (Jer. xxxi. 15; Matt. ii. 18).

Later, when Sargon's conquests of the Babylonians and Hittites had placed many bands of captives at his disposal, he brought into play that system of transportation which Assur-nazir-pal had perhaps been the first to institute. *And the king of Assyria brought men from Babylon, and from Cuthah, and from Ava, and from Hamath, and from Sepharvaim, and placed them in the cities of Samaria instead of the children of Israel: and they possessed Samaria, and dwelt in the cities thereof,* says the Book of Kings (2 K. xvii. 24).

"Distant Arab tribes," says the Assyrian

[1] Sayce, *Assyria,* 151.

monarch's inscription, "who inhabit the desert, of whom no scholar or envoy knew, and who had never brought their tribute to the kings my fathers, I slaughtered in the service of Assur, and transported what was left of them, setting them

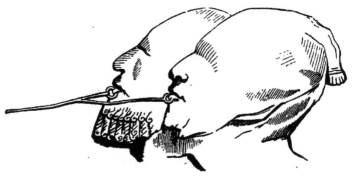

CAPTIVES OF SARGON.—After Rawlinson (Murray).

in the city of Samaria," in the "midst of the land of Beth-Omri." [1]

This importation of despised "Arab" tribes, who came *every nation with gods of their own*, and demanded from their master one of the captive priests of Jehovah to *teach them the manner of the god of the land*, was naturally abhorrent to the Jews. "*Unto this day*," says the writer of Kings, "*they do after the former manners.*"

The deportation of the inhabitants of Samaria

[1] Sayce, *Assyria*, 151.

had by no means been complete; only the heads of the nation had been taken away, and the remnant who were left soon intermixed with and dominated the foreign settlers. The little dwindling community who still worship in their humble synagogue at the foot of Mount Gerizim—" the oldest and the smallest sect in the world "[1]—still look upon themselves as the true descendants of Jacob and Joseph. But to the Jews they were neither Jew nor Gentile. The old feud between Judah and Israel, *the adversaries of Judah and Benjamin* (Ezra iv. 1), was now intensified by Jewish exclusiveness; and seven centuries after the time of Sargon, the bitterest taunt which Jewish malignity could level at our Lord was, " *Thou art a Samaritan and hast a devil* " (John viii. 48). We see the same feeling in the wondering inquiry of the woman of Samaria, " *How is it that thou, being a Jew, askest drink of me, which am a woman of Samaria? for the Jews have no dealings with the Samaritans* " (John iv. 9), and in the refusal of the Samaritan village to *receive Him, because His face was as though He would go to Jerusalem*

---

[1] Stanley, *Sinai and Palestine*, 240. They were in 1889 less than 150 in number.

(Luke ix. 53). We see it no less plainly in the parable of the good Samaritan, and in the gracious singling out of the Samaritan leper, who alone of the ten *returned to give glory to God* (Luke xvii.).

The Jews, the men of Judah, endured as a nation, and after the fall of Samaria gathered to themselves the whole of the national spirit. From this time forth, only, does it become possible to speak of Jewish tenacity, of Jewish steadfastness and valour.[1]

"At the Ethnic judgment seat," the Eldest of the Three tells Wilhelm Meister, "at the judgment seat of the God of nations, it is not asked Whether this is the best, the most excellent nation, but whether it lasts, whether it has continued. The Israelitish people . . . possesses few virtues, and most of the faults of other nations; but in cohesion, steadfastness, valour, and when all this would not serve, in obstinate toughness, it has no match. It is the most perseverant nation in the world: it is and was and will be, to glorify the name of

---

[1] "Only by an anachronism," says Dean Stanley, "do we apply the words Jew and Jewish to times before the overthrow of Samaria" (*Jewish Church*, ii. 382). The word Jew first occurs in the historical books, 2 Kings xvi. 6; in the Prophets, Jeremiah xxxii. 12.

Jehovah, through all ages. We have set it up, therefore, as the pattern figure; as the main figure, to which the others only serve as a frame."[1]

Samaria taken, her king *cut off, as the foam upon the water* (Hos. x. 7), Sargon turned his attention to the other rebels against his power. Babylonia, which had revolted on the death of Tiglath-Pileser III., had been invaded, and occupied by Merodach-Baladan, chief of the tribe called Chaldees (Caldai), who dwelt in the marshes near the Persian Gulf. Elam was threatening invasion; Hamath, encouraged by Egypt, had revolted, and had been joined by the Syrian cities, Arpad and Damascus. But soon, though the Chaldean was not dislodged from Babylon, all invaders were driven back; the frontier of Assyria was secured; Hamath was burnt to the ground; and Sargon, marching to the south, attacked the Philistine cities, and defeated the allied armies of Egypt and Philistia in a great pitched battle at Raphia.[2] With the

---

[1] Carlyle, *Trans. of the Wanderjahre*, ch. xi.

[2] In 719 B.C. The very lump of clay which received the impression of the treaty then concluded was found by Sir A.

defeat of the Pharaoh Sabako ended any real hope of defence from Egypt against Assyrian invasions.

The only formidable power which could still withstand the Assyrians was the Hittite empire—that empire which had contended with Sargon's great predecessor, first of the name, some 3000 years before ; and which had treated on equal terms with Rameses II. of Egypt, as with Tiglath-Pileser I. of Assyria. They had been a people before Abraham went forth from Ur of the Chaldees, and they only yielded to the arms of Assyria after the Israelites had been swept from Samaria.[1] Four years after the taking of Samaria, Carchemish also fell, and the Hittites disappear from history ; but the "maneh of Carchemish" continued long after to be a standard of weight in Assyrian contract-tables, and to attest the place which the Hittite capital once held in the world of commerce; and day by day scholars are beginning to realise more and more how vast was once the extent of Hittite dominion, and how great their importance in ancient history.

Layard at Nineveh, and is now in the British Museum.—Rawlinson, *Egypt*, 327.

[1] Wright, *Empire of Hittites*, 123.

*From the wilderness and this Lebanon even
unto the great river, the river Euphrates, all the
land* once belonged to the Hittites (Josh. i. 4).
At the mere rumour that the king of Israel
had *hired against* them the *kings of the Hittites
and the kings of the Egyptians*, the Syrians had
once abandoned a siege of Samaria on the very eve
of victory. *They arose and fled in the twilight, and
left their tents, and their horses, and their asses,
even the camp as it was, and fled for their life*
(2 Kings vii. 7).

Now Hittite and Syrian and Israelitish cities
alike lay bound at the feet of Sargon. *"Are not
my princes altogether kings?"* he was able to say.
*"Is not Calno as Carchemish? is not Hamath as
Arpad? is not Samaria as Damascus? . . . Shall
I not, as I have done unto Samaria and her idols,
so do to Jerusalem and her idols?"*

The wound of Israel was *incurable*; the turn
had *come unto Judah*; at the very gate of her
people, even at Jerusalem, stood the Assyrian
conqueror (Micah i. 9).

While Palestine was quiet, indeed, and Hezekiah
(who had succeeded his father Ahaz) continued to
pay the yearly tribute, Sargon devoted himself to

wars elsewhere. It is difficult not to connect with Hezekiah and the prosperous opening of his reign that message of peace and *goodwill toward men* which Isaiah had delivered to King Ahaz.[1] No doubt to his generation his reign seemed the fulfilment of that wonderful prophecy, which has come down to us through the ages :—

For unto us a child is born, unto us a son is given; and the government shall be upon his shoulder: and his name shall be called Wonderful, Counsellor, The mighty God, The everlasting Father, The Prince of Peace. Of the increase of his government and peace there shall be no end, upon the throne of David, and upon his kingdom, to order it, and to establish it with judgment and with justice from henceforth even for ever. The zeal of the Lord of hosts will perform this (Is. ix. 6).

During the first few years of Hezekiah's reign his land had peace. He instituted great reforms in her religion, breaking the images and cutting down the groves which had been the signs of her idolatry; he fostered her literary life, so that it is to the

---

[1] "There is a strong Jewish tradition that Hezekiah applied to himself, not only the predictions of Isaiah, but the 20th and 110th Psalms."—Stanley, *Jewish Church*, ii. 461.

records *which the men of Hezekiah, king of Judah,
copied out* [1] that we owe much of our Hebrew Bible.
*And the Lord was with him; and he prospered
whithersoever he went forth . . . After him was
none like him among all the kings of Judah, nor
any that were before him* (2 Kings xviii. 7, 5).

But this peaceful activity was soon to have an
end. About 712 Merodach-Baladan, the Chaldean
king, foreseeing that Babylon would be the conqueror's next victim, set about forming an alliance
against Sargon.

Taking as his pretext an illness from which
Hezekiah had lately recovered—

"At that time Merodach-Baladan, the son of Baladan,
king of Babylon, sent letters and a present to Hezekiah;
for he had heard that he had been sick, and was recovered.
And Hezekiah was glad of them, and shewed them the
house of his precious things, the silver, and the gold, and

---

[1] Proverbs xxv. 1. "Il y a deux livres d'enfants par excellence, Homère et la Bible."—Renan, *Hist. du Peuple d'Is.*
ii. 217. "Ce n'était pas un livre sacerdotal, c'était un livre
national. Ces histoires furent héroïques et populaires, avant
d'être sacrées. Le mot profane serait ici fort déplacé; car ce
mot n'a de sens que par son opposition à ce qui est devenu
religieux. La distinction des deux vies n'était pas faite. . . .
Certes Iahvé remplissait déjà ces vieux récits; mais les dieux
remplissent aussi l'Iliade et l'Odyssée sans que pour cela l'Iliade
et l'Odyssée soient des livres sacrés."—*Ib.* ii. 237.

the spices, and the precious ointment, and all the house
of his armour, and all that was found in his treasures :
there was nothing in his house, nor in all his dominion,
that Hezekiah shewed them not. Then came Isaiah the
prophet unto king Hezekiah, and said unto him, What
said these men ? and from whence came they unto
thee ? And Hezekiah said, They are come from a far
country unto me, even from Babylon.   Then said he,
What have they seen in thine house ? And Hezekiah
answered, All that is in mine house have they seen :
there is nothing among my treasures that I have not
shewed them. Then said Isaiah to Hezekiah, Hear the
word of the Lord of hosts : Behold, the days come, that
all that is in thine house, and that which thy fathers
have laid up in store until this day, shall be carried
to Babylon : nothing shall be left, saith the Lord " (Is.
xxxix. ; 2 Kings xx.).

Hezekiah seemed to acquiesce; nevertheless
he allied himself with Yavan, "the Greek," newly
appointed king of Ashdod, and with Moab and
Edom, and sent an embassy begging for help from
the king of Egypt. *And in that day did the Lord
God of hosts call to weeping, and to mourning, and
to baldness, and to girding with sackcloth: and
behold joy and gladness, slaying oxen and killing
sheep, eating flesh and drinking wine: let us eat
and drink, for to-morrow we shall die* (Is. xxii.
12, 13).

Sabako was again ready enough with promises;

but before his help, even had it been forthcoming, could reach the confederates, the Assyrian was upon them.

SARGON IN HIS WAR-CHARIOT (KHORSABAD).—After Rawlinson (Murray).

As usual he came *with speed swiftly :* none was weary nor stumbled amongst them ; none slumbered nor slept ; their arrows were sharp, and all their bows were bent ; their horses' hoofs were *counted like flint, and their wheels like a whirlwind* (Isaiah v. 26-28).

He is come to Aiath, he is passed to Migron ; at Michmash he hath laid up his carriages : they are gone over the passage : they have taken up their lodging at Geba ; Ramah is afraid ; Gibeah of Saul is fled. . . . Madmenah is removed ; the inhabitants of Gebim gather themselves to flee (Isaiah x. 28-31). Haste and terror are in the lines : and meanwhile Egypt makes no sign.

The Tartan, or commander-in-chief, was despatched by Sargon to lay siege to Ashdod ; Yavan was "overwhelmed by the fear of Asshur, and to the border of Egypt he fled away ";[1] "the wide-

[1] Sayce, *Assyria,* 152. The siege of Ashdod is the only occasion on which Sargon's name is mentioned in the Bible. For twenty-five centuries the passage of Isaiah (xx. 1) was absolutely the only evidence that such a monarch had ever existed. But the excavations of M. Botta (begun in 1842), and later those of Sir A. H. Layard, brought to light his annals ; and it is now recognised that chapters x. and xi. of Isaiah, as well as chapters xviii. to xx. and xxii., belong to this expedition of Sargon, and not to the later expedition of Sennacherib. For

spreading land of Judah " was overrun ; Jerusalem was taken; not for the last time were her people *afraid and ashamed of Ethiopia their expectation, and of Egypt their glory* (Isaiah xx. 5).

"In my ninth expedition and eleventh year, the people of the Philistines, Judah, Edom, and Moab, who dwell by the sea, who owed tribute and presents to Assur my lord, plotted rebellion," says Sargon's own record of the campaign; "men of insolence, who in order to revolt against me carried their bribes for alliance to Pharaoh king of Egypt, a prince who could not save them, and sent him homage." [1]

" *Woe to the land shadowing with wings, which* Sennacherib advanced from Lachish in the south-west ; not along the north-east road, which led past Nob. The invader is represented as lying at Nob on the very day when the oracle is spoken, for "that day" in x. 32 should be translated "to-day." Moreover the achievements of which he makes his boast, the conquest of Carchemish, Hamath, Arpad, Samaria, and Damascus, were all achievements of Sargon, not of his less warlike son.

"Ten years, therefore, before the campaign of Sennacherib, Jerusalem had felt the presence of an Assyrian army, a fact which serves to explain how it is that ' the fourteenth' year of Hezekiah has slipped into the text in Isaiah xxxvi. 1 (2 Kings xviii. 13) in place of ' the twenty-fourth.' "—Sayce, *Isaiah*, 60. See also his *Fresh Light*, 137 ; and Smith, *Assyria*, 113.

[1] Sayce, *Isaiah*, 92, 93.

O

is beyond the rivers of Ethiopia," cried the prophet :
*" that sendeth ambassadors by the sea, even in vessels
of bulrushes upon the waters, saying, Go, ye swift
messengers, to a nation scattered and peeled, to a
people terrible from their beginning hitherto; a
nation meted out and trodden down, whose land the
rivers have spoiled !"* (Is. xviii. 1, 2).

The rest of the reign of Sargon was occupied
with wars against Merodach-Baladan, and against
the king of Elam. In 705 he was murdered in
his new city of Dur-sargina, and was succeeded
by his son Sennacherib—not apparently the eldest
of the princes, for the name means "The Moon-
god has increased the Brethren."

Again, with a change of ruler, the conquered
provinces of Assyria broke into revolt; and, again
encouraged by Egypt, Hezekiah put himself at
the head of a confederacy which included
Phoenicia, Moab, and Edom. In vain did Isaiah
protest against his embassy to Zoan : as the
father had turned for help to Assyria thirty
years before, so did the son turn for help to
Egypt now.

"Woe to the rebellious children, saith the Lord," cried
the prophet, "that take counsel, but not of me ; and that

cover with a covering, but not of my Spirit, that they may
add sin to sin : that walk to go down into Egypt, and have
not asked at my mouth ; to strengthen themselves in the
strength of Pharaoh, and to trust in the shadow of Egypt !
Therefore shall the strength of Pharaoh be your shame,
and the trust in the shadow of Egypt your confusion. . . .
For the Egyptians shall help in vain, and to no purpose :
. . . For thus saith the Lord God, the Holy One of Israel ;
In returning and rest shall ye be saved ; in quietness and
in confidence shall be your strength : and ye would not.
But ye said, No ; for we will flee upon horses ; therefore
shall ye flee : and, We will ride upon the swift ; therefore
shall they that pursue you be swift" (Isaiah xxx.).

"Woe to them that go down to Egypt for help ; and
stay on horses, and trust in chariots, because they are
many ; and in horsemen, because they are very strong ;
but they look not unto the Holy One of Israel, neither
seek the Lord. . . . Now the Egyptians are men, and not
God ; and their horses flesh, and not spirit" (Isaiah xxxi.
1-3).

The Egyptians did indeed this time send their
horses and chariots to the relief of their ally ; but
the Assyrian was as usual beforehand with them.
Sennacherib quickly settled with his other enemies;
the year 701 found him on the march towards the
West, and soon nearly the whole of Palestine was
at his feet.

Sennacherib, king of Assyria, came "*up against
all the fenced cities of Judah, and took them,*" says
the Book of Kings (2, xviii. 13).

"*By the multitude of my chariots,*" Isaiah makes him say, "*am I come up to the height of the mountains, to the sides of Lebanon ; and I will cut down the tall cedars thereof, and the choice fir trees thereof : and I will enter into the height of his border, and the forest of his Carmel. I have digged, and drunk water ; and with the sole of my feet have I dried up all the rivers of the besieged places*" (Isaiah xxxvii. 24, 25). Vividly does his description of himself upon his monuments recall the words.

"The great king, the powerful king," he calls himself, "the king of nations, the king of Assyria, the king of the Four Regions, the diligent ruler, the favourite of the great gods, the observer of sworn faith, the guardian of the law, the embellisher of public buildings, the noble hero, the strong warrior, the first of kings, the punisher of unbelievers, the destroyer of wicked men."[1]

Among the mountains of Lebanon, in the valley of the Dog River, where the inscriptions of four empires meet, Sennacherib carved his memorial, side by side with the Hittite figure which Herodotus professed himself to have seen, and

[1] Rawlinson, *Ancient Monarchies*, ii. 456.

which (followed by every writer since his time) he called the Sesostris (ii. § 106).

Among the bas-reliefs discovered by Sir A. Layard at Nineveh are some representing the siege of Lachish. We see the city, with its battlements and towers, the banks thrown up against it, the besiegers, the kneeling archers in the front rank, and men with large ladles pouring water upon the flaming brands hurled from the walls above. In the foreground sits Sennacherib, on a throne of state, the royal feet resting upon a high footstool fashioned like the throne; the royal eyes complacently fixed upon the prisoners, some of whom are crouching before him, while two, already in the hands of the torturers, lie stretched naked on the ground to be flayed alive. Above the throne is an inscription telling that this is " Sennacherib, the mighty king, king of the country of Assyria, sitting on the throne of judgment before the city of Lachish." [1]

Here, then, we have a confirmation, almost startling in its horrible details, of the power and ferocity of the monarch to whom Hezekiah sent *to*

---

[1] Layard, *Nineveh and Babylon*, 149-152. In British Museum. Sayce, *Fresh Light,* 144.

Lachish, saying in terror, "*I have offended ; return from me : that which thou puttest on me will I bear*" (2 Kings xviii. 14).

Nothing would serve the Assyrian king but unconditioned surrender. Dividing his forces into two bands, he sent one to besiege Jerusalem, while the other met and routed the forces of Tirhakah [1] at Eltekeh. In his annals we have the history of the campaign, or of so much of it as was considered to redound to his glory.

"The priests, the chief men, and the common people of Ekron, who had thrown into chains their king, Padi, because he was faithful to his oaths to Assyria, and had given him up to Hezekiah, the Jew, who imprisoned him in hostile fashion, in a dark dungeon, feared in their hearts. The king of Egypt, the bowmen, the chariots, and the horses of the king of Ethiopia had gathered together innumerable forces and gone to their assistance. In the sight of the town of Eltekeh was their order of battle drawn up ; they summoned their troops to the battle. Trusting in Assur, my lord, I fought with them and overthrew them. . . . As for Hezekiah of Judah, who had not sub-

---

[1] Who had succeeded Sabako upon the throne of Egypt.

mitted to my yoke, forty-six of his strong cities, together with innumerable fortresses and small towns which depended on them, by overthrowing the walls and open attack, by battle, engines, and battering rams, I besieged, I captured. I brought out from the midst of them and counted as a spoil 200,150 persons, great and small, male and female, horses, mules, asses, camels, oxen and sheep without number. Hezekiah himself I shut up like a bird in a cage, in Jerusalem, his royal city. I built a line of forts against him, and I kept back his heel from going forth out of the great gate of his city."

The confusion that reigned in Jerusalem is graphically described by Isaiah. It was *as with the people, so with the priest ; as with the servant, so with his master ; as with the maid, so with her mistress ; as with the buyer, so with the seller ; as with the lender, so with the borrower ; as with the taker of usury, so with the giver of usury to him* (Is. **xxiv**. 2).

The city was *wholly gone up to the housetops*, anxiously scanning the horizon for the help that did not come. It was *a day of trouble, and of treading down, and of perplexity by the Lord God of hosts* (**xxii**. 1, 5).

In the midst of the confusion came the chiefs
of the besieging army—the Tartan or commander-
in-chief, the Rabsaris or chamberlain, the Rabshakeh (Rab-saki, vizier)—with their insulting
message to the defenders. Did they trust in
Egypt ? Behold Egypt was a *broken reed,*[1] *whereon
if a man lean it will go into his hand and pierce it.*
Did they trust in their God ? Had not Hezekiah
the reformer removed his *high places,* and broken
in pieces his brazen serpent ? Did they trust in
their own numbers ? The king of Assyria would
give them *two thousand horses,* if they on their
part were able *to set riders upon them.*[2]

There was no longer a powerful party advocat-
ing an Egyptian alliance, within the walls of
Jerusalem. The friends of Egypt had been
crushed when Tirhakah's army was crushed at
Eltekeh : they had been overwhelmed when the
Lord brought *upon them the waters of the river,
strong and many, even the king of Assyria, and all
his glory* (Isaiah viii. 7). Shebna the scribe—the
upstart, against whom (as representing a policy)

[1] The emblem of the king of Upper Egypt was the bent
stalk of a Nile water-reed.—King, *Cleopatra's Needle,* 71.
[2] 2 Kings xviii ; Isaiah xxxvi.

Isaiah's only personal prophecy had been uttered
(Is. xxii.),—Shebna had fallen ; and it was Eliakim
into whose hand the government had been committed, Eliakim who answered the Assyrian from
the wall. Fearing the effect of their confident
boasts upon the spirit of the people, he begged
them to speak *in the Syrian language*—the Aramaic,
which had become the common tongue of trade
and diplomacy, and was used by all educated
classes of that day, but which was not yet, as it
became after the Captivity, the common speech of
the Jews.[1]

Not only could every educated Assyrian of
the day speak Aramaic, but we also know from
the monuments that he was expected to read

[1] On the return from the captivity, Aramaic had become so
much the language of the Jews, that when Ezra the scribe,
standing upon his pulpit of wood *in the street that was before
the water-gate*, read to the assembled people the Hebrew book
of the Law of Moses, he was obliged to *give the sense*, so as to
cause them *to understand the reading* (Nehemiah viii. 1-8).
Aramaic was the common language of Palestine in the time of
our Lord — the language in which the few of his words
preserved to us in their original form appear to have been
spoken. The expression " one jot or one tittle " goes to prove
this, for Yod (the letter y) was the very smallest letter in the
Aramaic writing, whereas in the ancient Hebrew it was the
largest.—P. J. Smyth, *Old Documents and New Bible*, pp. 5-61.

and write Accadian, the old dead language of the Babylonians. To these two languages the Rabshakeh added the accomplishment of speaking Hebrew, in such a manner that the *men who sat upon the wall* of Jerusalem could understand his master's appeal: and the fact gives us a high idea of the education of the age.

To the answer sent by Hezekiah, a second insulting message was returned in writing by the Assyrian king; this time from Libnah, for Lachish had already fallen. But now Isaiah delivered his first message of consolation: *Thus saith the Lord concerning the king of Assyria, He shall not come into this city, nor shoot an arrow there, nor come before it with shields, nor cast a bank against it. By the way that he came, by the same shall he return, and shall not come into this city, saith the Lord. For I will defend this city, to save it, for mine own sake, and for my servant David's sake* (Isaiah xxxvii. 33-35).

Of the sudden reversal of fortune which then overtook the Assyrian army we find no mention on Assyrian monuments; but equally there is the tacit acknowledgment that the city Jerusalem was not taken. Never does an Assyrian monarch admit in his annals that a disaster or even a check has happened to himself or to his generals. Sometimes there is a mention of a defeat sustained by a former monarch ; sometimes we can only infer that the Assyrian arms were unsuccessful because no success is recorded, or because the expeditions against this or that country come to a sudden end, for no apparent reason. In the case of Sennacherib's army we gather that he did not capture Jerusalem, and that he made no more expeditions into Judea. For the details of his defeat we must not look to the royal records.

The story told to Herodotus, by his priestly informants in Egypt, was that Sethos, one of the kings of Lower Egypt, finding it impossible to get the soldiers to help him, because he had " despised and neglected the warrior class," collected an army of " traders, artisans, and market people," and marched against Sennacherib. " As the two armies lay opposite each other, there came in the night a multitude of field-mice, which devoured all the quivers and bowstrings of the enemy, and all the thongs by which they managed their shields. Next morning they began their flight, and great multitudes fell, as they had no arms wherewith to defend themselves. There stands to this day in the Temple of Vulcan a stone statue of Sethos, with a mouse in his hand, and an inscription to this effect—Look on me, and learn to reverence the Gods!" (ii. § 141).

Then the angel of the Lord went forth, says the Bible story, *and smote in the camp of the Assyrians a hundred and fourscore and five thousand: and when they arose early in the morning, behold, they were all dead corpses. So Sennacherib king of Assyria departed, and went and returned, and dwelt at Nineveh. He returned with shame of face to his own land. Behold at eveningtide trouble; and before the morning he is not.*[1]

To the Jews it seemed as if the Lord himself had stretched out his hand. " *The Lord of hosts is with us,*" they cried ; and their psalms of thankfulness have echoed through the ages since. The thought of that deliverance cheered Judas Maccabæus in his struggle against Antiochus:[2] the story of it is still read in the churches of Moscow on the anniversary of the retreat of the French from Russia; and the Hebrew psalm of praise

---

[1] Isaiah xxxvii. 36 ; 2 Chron. xxxii. 21 ; Is. xvii. 14, xxxi.

[2] 1 Maccabees vii. 41.

which begins "*God is our refuge and strength*" (xlvi.) forms the basis of the hymn "Ein' feste Burg ist unser Gott," which since Luther's time has been the rallying cry of Protestant Germany.[1]

Everybody knows the lines in which, as Dean Stanley has said, "one of the least religious of English poets, by the mere force of kindred genius, has so entirely, though unconsciously, absorbed into his Hebrew melody the minutest allusions of the contemporary prophets and psalmists, as to make it a fit conclusion for the whole event" (ii. 484).

' The Assyrian came down like the wolf on the fold,
  And his cohorts were gleaming in purple and gold ;[2]
  And the sheen of their spears was like stars on the sea,
  When the blue wave rolls nightly on deep Galilee.

' Like the leaves of the forest [3] when summer is green,
  That host with their banners at sunset were seen :

---

[1] Stanley, *Jewish Church*, ii. 483, 484.

[2] " Clothed with blue, captains and rulers, all of them desirable young men, horsemen riding upon horses" (Ezek. xxiii. 6) ; "clothed most gorgeously " (12).

[3] "Behold, the Assyrian was a cedar in Lebanon with fair branches. . . . Thus was he fair in his greatness, in the length of his branches " (Ezek. xxxi. 3-7).

Like the leaves of the forest when autumn hath blown,
That host on the morrow lay withered and strown.[1]

"For the angel of Death spread his wings on the blast,[2]
And breathed in the face of the foe as he passed ;
And the eyes of the sleepers waxed deadly and chill,
And their hearts but once heaved, and for ever grew
    still !

"And there lay the steed [3] with his nostril all wide,
But through it there rolled not the breath of his pride :
And the foam of his gaspiug lay white on the turf,
And cold as the spray of the rock-beating surf.

.   .   .   .   .

"And the tents were all silent, the banners alone,
The lances unlifted, the trumpet unblown.

.   .   .   .   .

"And the might of the Gentile, unsmote by the sword,
Hath melted like snow in the glance of the Lord !" [4]

Sennacherib came no more into the land of
Israel. We do not hear of any other campaigns

---

[1] "Behold at eveningtide trouble ; and before the morning
he is not" (Isaiah xvii. 14).

[2] "The angel of the Lord went forth" (Is. xxxvii. 36).
"Behold, I will send a blast upon him" (7).

[3] "The stouthearted are spoiled, they have slept their sleep.
. . . At thy rebuke, O God of Jacob, both the chariot and
horse are cast into a dead sleep . . . the earth feared, and was
still" (Ps. lxxvi. 5-8).

[4] "The heathen raged, the kingdoms were moved: he
uttered his voice, the earth melted" (Ps. xlvi. 6). Also Is.
xxxi. entire.

in the West, and the last twenty years of his life
were spent in constant wars with Babylonia.
Babylon was at last taken and completely sacked,
and the Chaldeans were pursued and defeated in
their own marshes by the Persian Gulf.

Sennacherib also did much to beautify his
capital, and the monuments of the latter part of
his reign often represent him standing in his
chariot, watching the gangs of captive labourers
who are yoked together sometimes by a bar
fastened to the waist, sometimes by fetters round
their ankles, while they toil at the vast walls of
Nineveh or drag into place the colossal bulls and
dragons which adorned her palaces.[1]

In 681 Sennacherib was murdered, *as he was
worshipping in the house of his god,* by his elder
sons, Assur-mulik and Nergal-shareser; *and Esar-
haddon his son reigned in his stead* (2 Kings
xix. 37). The brothers may perhaps have been

---

[1] Rawlinson, *Ancient Monarchies,* ii. 463 ; Smith, *Assyria,*
135. Layard finds much analogy between the palace-temples
of Sennacherib and the temple of Solomon, and indeed thinks
with Mr. Fergusson that the actual remains at Nineveh do
much to illustrate and explain the Jewish temple, of which not
a fragment remains to guide us through the intricacies of the
Hebrew architectural description.—*Nineveh and Babylon,* 155,
186, 192, 606, 642 ; *Bible Dict.* ii. 659.

INTERIOR OF AN ASSYRIAN PALACE RESTORED.—After Rawlinson (Murray).

jealous of the favour shown to Esar-haddon, of which there is curious evidence in the will of Sennacherib, now to be seen among the tablets in the British Museum.

"I, Sennacherib, king of multitudes, king of Assyria, bequeath armlets of gold, quantities of ivory, a platter of gold, ornaments and chains for the neck, all these beautiful things of which there are heaps, and three sorts of precious stones, one and a half manehs, and two and a half shekels in weight, to Esar-haddon my son, whose name was afterwards changed to Assur-sar-illik by my wish."[1]

An inscription from Nineveh, also in the British Museum, is supposed to record the feelings with which Esar-haddon received the news of his father's murder. "I was angry in heart and my liver was inflamed with rage," he says. "For the ruling of my Father's House, and the assumption of my priesthood to Ashur, the Moon, the Sun, Bel, Nebo, Nergal, Istar of Nineveh and Istar of Arbela I lifted up my hands; and they granted my petition."

---

[1] Sayce, *Fresh Light*, 150. Mr. Pinches tells me, however, that this "will" is simply a deed of gift, the verb being *adin*, "I have given," not *uŝadgil*, "I have bequeathed."

P

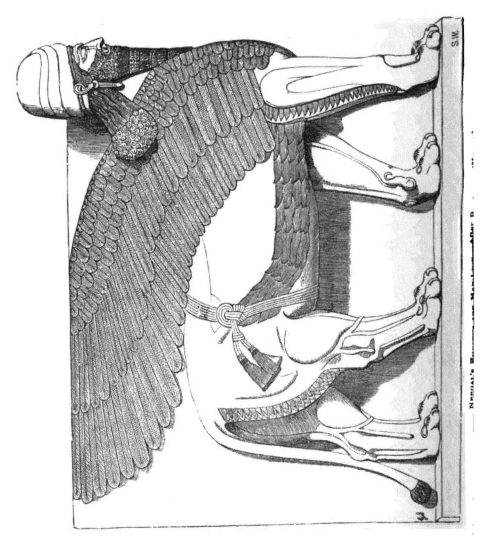

NINEVEH SCULPTURES AND MANNERS. After B

Esar-haddon proved himself a wise and politic ruler. Not only were his conquests very great, for he ruled from Babylonia to Egypt, "from the rising up of the sun to the going down of the same"; but he was the only king of Assyria who made any attempt to win the friendship of the nations he had conquered.

His first expedition was to Babylon, where the son of Merodach-Baladan had "taken the opportunity to rebel." Even after the time that the great gods "had me, Esar-haddon, on the throne of my Father happily seated, and the sovereignty of the land had given to me, even then he worshipped me not," says the inscription; "he gave me no more gifts, he would not do homage to me, and his envoy to my presence he would not send. He would not even inquire after the health of My Majesty" (*Rec.* iii. 105). But when the insurgent had been "slain with the sword," and his brother had kissed the conqueror's feet, Esar-haddon, in a spirit very different from that of his father, set about repairing some of the ravages which Sennacherib had caused. From that time he often held his court at Babylon; and this explains the fact (so long a stumbling-block to commentators) that when *the captains of the host of the king of Assyria* took prisoner Manasseh (the renegade son of Hezekiah), they carried him in his fetters *to Babylon,* and not to Nineveh.

In 676 Esar-haddon captured Sidon. "Conqueror of the city Sidon, which is on the sea, sweeper away of all its villages," says his inscription, "its citadel and residence I rooted up, and into the sea I flung them. . . . Men and women without number, oxen and sheep and mules, I swept them all off to Assyria." The same inscription relates that he "assembled twenty-two kings from the land of Syria, and of the sea-coast and the islands." And in another place we read among them the names of " Baal, king of Tyre ; and Manasseh, king of Judah."

It was in 674 that the great achievement of Esar-haddon's reign, the conquest of Egypt, was undertaken. The "burden" pronounced upon Egypt by Isaiah (xix.) must belong to this time —a time when the Egyptians were set *against the Egyptians,* and they fought *every one against his brother, and every one against his neighbour ; city against city, and kingdom against kingdom.* The whole country was divided into petty states,

warring among themselves, and threatened by the
Ethiopian Tirhakah from the south, and by the
Assyrian Esar-haddon from the north.   Even
when the whole country was given *over into the*
hand of the cruel lord from Assyria, the satraps
appointed by him quarrelled among themselves,
and again and again his armies were forced to
interfere.   But Esar-haddon kept his grip upon the
country, and after a glorious reign of thirteen years
he died "King of Assyria, Babylon, Egypt, Meroë,
and Ethiopia"; having "marched victorious without
a rival from the rising of the sun to the setting of
the sun." [1]

Just before his death he had associated with himself in the sovereignty his eldest son, Assur-bani-
pal, the "*great and noble Asnapper*" of Ezra (iv. 10).

Assur-bani-pal was he whom the Greeks called
Sardanapalus ; but he must in reality have been
a very different person from the effeminate volup-
tuary whom the Greek historian Diodorus has
described to us.   "Sardanapalus, the thirtieth from
Ninus, and the last king of the Assyrians, exceeded
all his predecessors in sloth and luxury," says Dio-

---

[1] The inscriptions of Esar-haddon here quoted are in *Records
of the Past*, iii. 103-120.

dorus, and "being thus corrupt in his morals, he not only came to a miserable end himself, but utterly overturned the Assyrian monarchy, which had continued longer than any we read of" (ii. 2).

As cruel as he was powerful, Assur-bani-pal is the very type and picture of an Assyrian monarch; and in many ways he seems to have been the greatest of them all. He was a munificent patron of literature, and added more to the royal library at Nineveh than any of the kings who had gone before him. In his day it is thought to have contained upwards of 30,000 clay tablets, treating of every branch of knowledge. His agents ransacked Babylonia for ancient texts, and these were all carefully classified and catalogued. Thus the series of tablets containing the account of the Creation, which begins with the phrase "Formerly that which is above was not yet called the Heaven," was ranged in order and docketed "Formerly that which is above No. 1," "Formerly that which is above No. 2," and so on,[1] while in many cases translations of the ancient Accadian texts were appended; and there are reading-books, word-lists, and lists of grammatical paradigms, etc.,

[1] Maspéro, *Ancient Egypt and Assyria*, 289.

of the Accadian language ; so that it is to Assur-
bani-pal that we owe much of our knowledge of
early Babylonian life and literature.[1]

The only representation that has come down
to us of an Assyrian queen belongs to the time of
Assur-bani-pal.   Richly attired, she sits in the
palace-garden, opposite her lord, who reclines
upon a couch ; they pledge one another out of
goblets, under the shade of the trees, while the
musicians play and the fan-bearers make cool
breezes.   Complete in its every detail, the picture
shows well the luxury and refinement of the time ;
it also shows with what barbarity such luxury and
refinement could co-exist, for behind the queen,
as she sits placidly quaffing her wine, hangs the
severed head of a captive, dangling in ghastly con-
trast among the festoons of the trellised bower above.[2]

---

[1] It is literally the fact that up to 1842, when M. Botta
undertook his first excavations, "a case three feet square en-
closed all that remained, not only of the great city Nineveh,
but of Babylon itself" (Layard, *Discoveries at Nineveh*, In-
trod.). M. Botta was ably followed by Sir A. H. Layard, and he
by others, so that we now possess an amount of Assyrian literature more than equal to that of the Hebrews as contained in
the Old Testament.

[2] Rawlinson, *Five Great Monarchies*, i. 494 ; Birch, *Assyria*,
194 ; Maspéro, *Ancient Egypt and Assyria*, 373.

Assur-bani-pal's love of sport is attested by many a bas-relief and inscription discovered at Nineveh, and by the very figures of his favourite hounds, which have been found modelled in

TORTURE OF CAPTIVES UNDER ASSUR-BANI-PAL.

clay, painted and inscribed each with its name. But he does not seem to have been so bold a sportsman or so hardy a warrior as his fathers before him, for his lion-hunts were not held in the open, but within the safe enclosure of the Royal Paradeisos or Parks ; and, if he ever accompanied his army in the field, he certainly took very little active part in its proceedings, only putting himself at the head of his troops when the day came for leading the triumphal march into Nineveh.

At first the veterans of Esar-haddon were able to keep and even to extend the empire which Assyria had won. Egypt revolted, but was re-conquered in two expeditions. Tirhakah was finally driven from the country, to die worn out by his long contest with the power of Assyria; Thebes, the once mighty capital of the Pharaohs, was plundered and destroyed, its temples hewn in pieces, its treasures carried away by the conquerors.

Exultingly Nahum, the last of the Israelitish prophets, pointed to her fall; exultingly he asked of her conquerors whether their strength was greater than once hers had been.[1] "*Art thou better than populous No, that was situate among the rivers, that had the waters round about it,*

---

[1] "The very date of his prophecy, so long disputed, can be fixed approximately by the reference it contains to the sack of No-Amon or Thebes (iii. 8). The prophecy was delivered hard upon sixty years before the fall of Nineveh, when the Assyrian empire was at the height of its prosperity, and mistress of the eastern world."—Sayce, *Assyria*, 15. (See Table, *infra*, p. 227.)

whose rampart was the sea, and her wall was from the sea? Ethiopia and Egypt were her strength, and it was infinite; Put and Lubim were thy helpers. Yet was she carried away, she went into captivity: her young children also were dashed in pieces at the top of all the streets: and they cast lots for her honourable men, and all her great men were bound in chains" (iii. 8-10).

Little less than sixty years later Nineveh too was to be laid waste, to be bruised with a bruise which there was *no healing* (iii. 19). Meanwhile, indeed, she seemed at the height of her power. Babylonia and Elam and Arabia lay vanquished at her feet; and from distant Lydia, away in the south-west corner of Asia Minor, a state whose very name had hitherto been unknown to the Assyrians, came at this time messengers, strangely dressed and speaking an unknown tongue, who brought word that Gyges their king had heard of the glories of Assyria and desired to make submission to her.

But in the midst of all this power and prosperity the great empire was crumbling to dust. Tirhakah, so long the adversary of the Assyrian power in Egypt, was dead; but his mantle had fallen upon

Psammetichus, king of Sais, one of the twelve princes who were ruling the Nile valley under Assyrian suzerainty. Herodotus tells how Psammetichus fulfilled the oracle which decreed that one among the twelve should become king of the whole land, how he was banished by his eleven rivals, and how he thereupon determined to make himself supreme over them and independent of Assyria. To effect this he called in the aid of the Greeks, under the Lydian Gyges, who, faithless to his proffered pledges, sent a force to aid in the revolt.

The oracle had told Psammetichus that " vengeance would come from the sea, when brazen men should appear." Now the brass-helmeted mercenaries of Greece made him sole master of Egypt, and drove out for ever the garrisons of Assyria, receiving as their reward " camps " on either side the Nile, and becoming " the parents of the whole class of interpreters in Egypt." Thus was the Nile valley lost for ever to Assyria, and thus was the China of the old world thrown open to the foreigner. " From the date of the original settlement of these persons in Egypt," says Herodotus, " we Greeks, through our intercourse with them, have acquired an

accurate knowledge of the several events in
Egyptian history, from the reign of Psammetichus
downwards ; but before his time no foreigners had
ever taken up their residence in that land"
(ii. § 154).

Not content with driving the Assyrians out of
the Nile valley, Psammetichus joined the great
league against the Assyrian power, which was
headed by the viceroy of Babylon (Assur-bani-pal's
own brother), and supported by the faithless
Gyges. From this time forth Assyria was con-
tending, not for dominion, but for very life. To
all her other enemies were added the Medes, who,
tributaries to Assyria in the days of her power,
had taken advantage of her weakness to organise
themselves into a rival empire, and were now on
the watch for an opportunity of matching themselves against her.

According to Herodotus, Cyaxares of Media had
actually begun the siege of Nineveh, when for a
time his hand was stayed by a great horde of
Scythians from beyond the Caucasus, who "burst
into Asia," and held all the countries round in
terror and subjection.[1]

---

[1] Herodotus, i. 106. Jer. i. 13, iv. 16, v. 15, vi. 22, and

It was one of those floods of barbarism which, from time to time, through all the course of ancient history, poured from the northern plains of Europe and Asia upon the more fertile and civilised regions of the south. As a gathering flood, as a *whirlwind, as a cloud to cover the land* they came, *with a great commotion out of the north country.* " Their dominion lasted," says Herodotus, " eight-and-twenty years, during which time their insolence and oppression spread ruin on every side."

But either their power spent itself by its very fury, or riot and luxury reduced their forces, for when they reached Palestine on their march towards the Nile, they allowed themselves to be bought off by the Egyptian king, who was at that time besieging Ashdod. "Psammetichus met them," says Herodotus, "with gifts and prayers, and prevailed on them to advance no farther." And finally " Cyaxares and the Medes invited the greater part of them to a banquet, and made them drunk with wine, after which they were all massacred."

Meanwhile Assur-bani-pal had died, and his

x. 17-25, as well as chaps. xxxviii. xxxix. of Ezekiel, are supposed to refer to these Scythic inroads.

successors had done nothing to restore the fallen glories of Assyria. There was now, moreover, no longer any foreign power to stand between Nineveh—*that great city*—and her doom. Not only was every country round her hostile, but Nabopolassar, the general whom the Assyrian king had sent to put down the latest Babylonian revolt, had turned his successful arms upon his master. In 610 he allied himself with Cyaxares, and, to cement their friendship, asked the hand of a Median princess for his son Nabu-kud-urri-uzur—the world-renowned Nebuchadnezzar of later days. The allies also asked and obtained the help of Necho, who had just succeeded his father Psammetichus upon the throne of Egypt, and who at once set forth upon his march through Palestine towards the Euphrates.

It was on his way to help his allies that Necho met and defeated Josiah of Judah, upon the plain of Megiddo—that battle-field of the ancient world which saw so many hard-fought fights as to become, in the minds of men, the type of the New Testament Armageddon, where the forces of good and evil would *gather them to the battle of the great day of God Almighty* (Rev. xvi. 16).

During all the troubled time through which the world had just been passing, Josiah (who had succeeded the wicked kings Manasseh and Amon upon the throne of Judah) had peacefully pursued the path of reform. He had even kept a passover, such as *there was not holden from the days of the judges that judged Israel, nor in all the days of the kings of Israel, nor of the kings of Judah.*

" In the eighteenth year of the reign of Josiah was this passover kept," says the chronicler. " But after all this, when Josiah had prepared the temple, Necho king of Egypt came up to fight against Carchemish by Euphrates : and Josiah (*faithful to his Assyrian suzerain*) went out against him. But he sent ambassadors to him, saying, What have I to do with thee, thou king of Judah ? I come not against thee this day, but against the house wherewith I have war. . . . Nevertheless Josiah would not turn his face from him, but disguised himself, that he might fight with him, and hearkened not unto the words of Necho from the mouth of God, and came to fight in the valley of Megiddo. And the archers shot at king Josiah : and the king said to his servants, Have me away ; for I am sore wounded. . . . And they brought him to Jerusalem, and he died, and was buried in one of the sepulchres of his fathers. And all Judah and Jerusalem mourned for Josiah " (2 Chron. xxxv. 19-24 ; 2 Kings xxiii.).

The way was cleared, and Necho marched on to Carchemish, the ancient Hittite capital, which he captured, thus severing the Assyrian territory at a blow; after which he claimed, as his share of the spoils, all the country between the Euphrates and the Nile.

Meanwhile the Medes and Babylonians were carrying on the siege of Nineveh. A desperate defence was made by the king, Sin-sarra-iskun, the Saracus of the Greeks. He trusted, says Diodorus,[1] in the fortifications of "*that great city*," which its founder, the mythical Ninus, had resolved on building—" of that state and grandeur, as should not only be the greatest then in the world, but such as none that ever should come after him should be able easily to exceed. . . . And the founder was not herein deceived, for none ever after built the like, either as to the largeness of its circumference, or the stateliness of its walls. For the wall was 100 feet in height, and so broad as three chariots might be driven together upon it abreast " (ii. 1).[2]

[1] The unreliability of Ctesias as quoted by Diodorus is shown by the fact that he confounds "Sardanapalus" with "Saracus," and makes Nineveh lie on the Euphrates instead of on the Tigris.

[2] "Xenophon, who passed close to the ruins on his retreat with the Ten Thousand, calls the height 150 feet, and the width 50 feet."—Rawlinson, *Five Great Monarchies*, i. 257.

The Assyrian king was moreover encouraged to withstand a siege, " for that he was acquainted with an antient prophecy 'that Nineveh could never be taken by force, till the river became the city's enemy.'" But "the third year it happened that the Euphrates, overflowing with continual rains, came up into a part of the city, and tore down the wall twenty furlongs in length. The king hereupon conceiving that the oracle was accomplished, in that the river was an apparent enemy to the city, utterly despaired ; and therefore, that he might not fall into the hands of his enemies, he caused a huge pile of wood to be made in his palace court, and heaped together upon it all his gold, silver, and royal apparel, and enclosing all his women and attendants in an apartment within the pile, caused it to be set on fire, and burnt himself and them together " (Diod. ii. 2).

Thus the *gates of the rivers* of Nineveh—the arrow-river Tigris and the Khusur—were *opened*, and the *palace dissolved*. Assyria was so wholly a military power, her history is so entirely the

---

"The remains still existing of these fortifications almost confirm the statements of Diodorus Siculus."—Layard, *Nineveh and Babylon*, 660.

history of her armies and her kings, that with the capture of her capital the whole nation was, as it were, blotted out of existence. Never has a great capital more entirely perished and disappeared. *With an overrunning flood the Lord made an utter end of the place thereof, and darkness pursued his enemies* (Nahum i. 8).

"Niniue," says an ancient traveller, "Niniue (that which God himself calleth that Great Citie) hath not one stone standing, which may giue memorie of the being of a towne."[1]

Desolation is in her thresholds. . . . This is the rejoicing city that dwelt carelessly, that said in her heart, I am, and there is none beside me: how is she become a desolation, a place for beasts to lie down in! every one that passeth by her shall hiss, and wag his hand (Zeph. ii. 15).

Empty and void and waste, her very site remained for centuries unknown, so that men asked themselves: *Where is the dwelling-place of the lions, and the feeding-place of the young lions, where the lion, even the old lion, walked, and the lion's whelp, and none made them afraid?* (Nahum ii. 11).

[1] Sir Anthony Shirley (1565-1630), *Travels in Persia.* Quoted by Layard, *Nineveh and Babylon,* 660.

CHRONOLOGICAL TABLE

1130.	**Tiglath-Pileser I.** founds first Assyrian empire.
1090.	Succeeded by Samas Rimmon (his brother).
883.	**Assur-nazir-pal** king.
858.	**Shalmaneser II.** (his son) king.
853-51.	Defeats Ahab and allies at Karkar. Death of Ahab.
850-43.	Campaigns against Hadadeser (Benhadad II.).
841.	Campaigns against Hazael. Tribute paid by Jehu.
745.	Pul (**Tiglath-Pileser III.**) usurps throne.
743-40.	Attacks Hittites. Uzziah submits.
738.	Receives tribute from Menahem and Rezin.
734.	Besieges Damascus. Carries off tribes beyond Jordan. Ahaz vassal.
733-32.	Substitutes Hoshea for Pekah, king of Israel. Damascus taken.
727.	**Shalmaneser V.** king.
722.	**Sargon** seizes throne. Takes Samaria.
721.	Merodach-Baladan conquers Babylon.
719.	Sargon conquers Hamath. Defeats Sabako (So) at Raphia.
712.	Merodach-Baladan sends embassy to Hezekiah.
711.	Sargon in Judah.
704.	**Sennacherib** king.
701.	Invades Judah. Battle of Eltekeh. Retreat.
681.	**Esar-haddon** king.
676.	Receives tribute of Manasseh. Conquers Egypt.
668.	**Assur-bani-pal** (Sardanapalus) king.
665.	Thebes (No-Amon) destroyed.
652.	Babylonia revolts.
? 630-10.	Scythian invasion.
? 607.	Nineveh taken.

CHAPTER V

THE fall of Nineveh was followed by a period of
peace—by a pause in the hurry of events. The
dominions of Assyria had been carved out among
her conquerors, and, for a time, each was occupied
within his own boundaries—Cyaxares in the
Median provinces of the north, Nabopolassar in
the south, and Necho in establishing his dominion
over all the tract that lay between the Nile on the
one hand and the Euphrates on the other. Not
only had Necho defeated and killed Josiah, but he
had carried off Josiah's successor, Jehoahaz or
Shallum, to Egypt, and had made another of the
princes [1] king in Jerusalem, *putting the land to a
tribute.*

[1] Eliakim, who, in accordance with what seems to have been
the custom of the time, on ascending the throne *turned his
name*, and took that of Jehoiakim. Jeremiah uses the name
Jehoiakim ; but he always speaks of Jehoahaz as Shallum, and
of Jehoiachin as Jeconiah or Coniah.

Nabopolassar was too busy strengthening his power in Babylonia to precipitate the inevitable quarrel; hence, for the time, Egypt was the greatest power in the Jewish world. For centuries she had not been so strong in Palestine as during these first three years of Necho's reign.

But the arrangement was one that could not last, and a great prophet, perhaps the greatest of all the seers of Israel, had arisen to show to the people of God the dangers of their way. He came as a *messenger* to kings and people, *rising up betimes* and warning them that unless they were wise—unless they repented them of their idolatrous ways, and submitted to the inevitable before it was too late—their city would be delivered over to the Babylonian, the conqueror of Assyria (2 Chron. xxxvi. 15).

But the people would not believe Jeremiah. To them Egypt seemed the power most to be feared, and, heedless of the doom that was hanging over his land, Jehoiakim taxed it *to give the money according to the commandment of Pharaoh: he exacted the silver and the gold of the people* (2 Kings xxv. 35); and, while they were groaning under

the load, he lavished money upon the adornment
of his palace.

Silver spread into plates is brought from Tarshish,
and gold from Uphaz, the work of the workman,
and of the hands of the founder : blue and purple is
their clothing : they are all the work of cunning men.
But the Lord is the true God, he is the living God,
and an everlasting king : at his wrath the earth
shall tremble, and the nations shall not be able to
abide his indignation (Jer. x. 9).

" Weep ye not for the dead," said the solemn voice of the
prophet. " Weep ye not for the dead, neither bemoan
him : but weep sore for him that goeth away : for he
shall return no more, nor see his native country. For
thus saith the Lord concerning Shallum the son of Josiah
king of Judah, which reigned instead of Josiah his father,
which went forth out of this place, He shall not return
thither any more : but he shall die in the place whither
they have led him captive, and shall see this land no
more.

" Woe unto him that buildeth his house by unrighteous-
ness, and his chambers by wrong ; that useth his neighbour's
service without wages, and giveth him not for his work ;
That saith, I will build me a wide house and large
chambers, and cutteth him out windows ; and it is .ceiled
with cedar, and painted with vermilion ! Shalt thou reign,
because thou closest thyself in cedar ? Did not thy father
eat and drink, and do judgment and justice, and then it
was well with him ? He judged the cause of the poor

and needy ; then it was well with him : was not this to
know me ? saith the Lord.

"But thine eyes and thine heart are not but for thy
covetousness, and for to shed innocent blood, and for
oppression, and for violence, to do it. Therefore thus
saith the Lord concerning Jehoiakim the son of Josiah
king of Judah, They shall not lament for him, saying,
Ah my brother ! or, Ah sister ! they shall not lament
for him, saying, Ah lord ! or, Ah his glory ! He shall be
buried with the burial of an ass, drawn and cast forth
beyond the gates of Jerusalem " (Jer. xxii. 10-19).

There was much in the circumstances surround-
ing Jeremiah that resembled those of Isaiah ;
but times had changed since the days of the
earlier prophet. On the one hand, Nebuchadnezzar
was a foe even more formidable than Sargon or
Sennacherib; and, on the other, Egypt was more
prepared to make a struggle for dominion in the
East.

The Jews, therefore, could not remain neutral;
they had the choice only of masters. But while
Jeremiah pressed upon them the need of submission
to the Chaldean, his adversaries, the priestly
party—the very representatives of the men who
had withstood Isaiah—now quoted against him
Isaiah's assurances that *in quietness and in confidence* should be their strength.

As in the days of Isaiah, Israel stood trembling between Chaldea on the one hand and Egypt on the other: again, *like a silly dove* she called first to Egypt and then to Assyria (Hosea vi. 8), fluttering with fear, as the net was spread more closely round her.[1] But whereas Isaiah a century earlier had bent all his energies to the task of making the people believe that the conqueror should not come into their city, it was now the task of Jeremiah to deliver to his generation exactly the opposite message.

In vain did the later prophet, standing in the accursed valley of Hinnom, soon to be called the *Valley of Slaughter*, break in pieces the potter's earthen vessel in the sight of the *ancients of the people and of the ancients of the priests*, saying," *Thus saith the Lord of hosts, Even so will I break this people and this city, as one breaketh a potter's vessel, that cannot be made whole again* " (Jer. xix. 11).

Even when the news came that the unnatural alliance between Egypt and Babylonia had been shattered, and that Pharaoh Necho had gone up to

---

[1] The simile of the outspread net occurs over and over again in the prophets of the time. See Ezek. xii. 13, xvii. 20, xxxii. 3 ; Hab. i. 15-17.

battle against his Babylonian allies, Jehoiakim refused to bow to the inevitable.

It was *the day of the Lord God of hosts, a day of vengeance that he may avenge him of his adversaries.* "*The Lord God of hosts hath a sacrifice in the north country, by the river Euphrates,*" said the prophet. The Egyptian army, rising like a river in flood, with tributaries from all its subject nations—*Ethiopians and the Libyans, that handle the shield; and the Lydians that handle and bend the bow*—was driven back upon itself. The shock of its defeat was felt throughout the world. *The nations have heard of thy shame, and thy cry hath filled the land : for the mighty man hath stumbled against the mighty, and they are fallen both together. . . . Pharaoh king of Egypt is but a noise ; he hath passed the time appointed* (Jer. xlvi.).

Nabopolassar, king of Babylon, says the Chaldean chronicler (as quoted by Josephus), "sent his son Nabuchodonosor with a great army against Egypt, and against Judea, upon his being informed that they had revolted from him ; and by that means he subdued them all, and set fire to the temple that was at Jerusalem, and removed our people entirely out of their own country, and transferred them to Babylon; and it happened that our city was desolate during the interval of seventy years, until the days of Cyrus king of Persia."

Thus began the Babylonian captivity. Among those whom the conqueror carried away were hostages *of the king's seed, and of the princes, children in whom was no blemish, but well-favoured, and skilful,* with whom were Daniel and his companions (Dan. i.).

Nebuchadnezzar himself was pushing on to Egypt, when "it came to pass that his father, Nabopolassar, was seized with a disorder which proved fatal, and he died in the city of Babylon, after he had reigned nine-and-twenty years." [1] "After a short time Nabuchodonosor, receiving the intelligence of his father's death, set the affairs of Egypt and the other countries in order, and committed the captives he had taken from the Jews and Phoenicians and Syrians, and of the nations belonging to Egypt, to some of his friends, that they might conduct that part of the forces that had on heavy armour, with the rest of his baggage, to Babylonia; while he went in haste, with a few followers, across the desert to Babylon;

[1] Berosus, from Josephus, Cont. Ap.; Cory, 38.

where, when he was come, he found that affairs had
been well conducted by the Chaldeans,[1] and that
the principal person among them had preserved
the kingdom for him : accordingly he now obtained
possession of all his father's dominions.   And he
ordered the captives to be distributed in colonies
in the most proper places of Babylonia; and
adorned the temple of Belus, and the other temples,
in a sumptuous and pious manner, out of the spoils
he had taken in this war.   He also rebuilt the old
city."

For the next few years Nebuchadnezzar appears

---

[1] The name "Chaldean" is used by ancient writers in a
double sense. Sometimes it is used instead of Assyrian or
Babylonian, and applies to the whole nation; sometimes it
refers to a certain order or sect within the nation, the "*wise
men of Babylon*" as they are called throughout the book of
Daniel—the class whom Herodotus (in the time of Xerxes)
called Chaldeans and regarded as priests (ii. 181). "It was,"
says Grote, "the paramount ascendency of this order which
seems to have caused the Babylonian people generally to be
spoken of as Chaldeans" (*Hist.* iii. 392).

The real Chaldeans—the Caldai—are not mentioned on any
known monument before 879 B.C. Under Merodach-Baladan
they captured Babylon in the first year of Sargon, 722 B.C., and
from that time forward the country became known as Chaldea.
But the Chaldean *people* of the Bible is merely a translation of
the word Casdim, in all likelihood the Assyrian *Casidu*, "conqueror."—Smith, *Babylonia*, 92-103.

to have stayed quietly at Babylon, busy in planning the great buildings which (even more than his conquests of foreign nations) were the glory of his reign ; but soon (602 B.C.) Jehoiakim, in spite of Jeremiah's warnings, began to waver in his allegiance to Babylon.

In vain did Jeremiah, from the hiding-place whither the intolerance of his enemies had driven him, send forth by the hand of Baruch a solemn written prophecy of the evil which was to come upon the land. When only three or four leaves of the epistle had been read before the king, sitting *in the winter-house,* he cut the rest *with the pen-knife, and cast it into the fire that was on the hearth, until all the roll was consumed* (Jer. xxxvi. 23).

" It was his last chance, his last offer of mercy : and as he threw the torn fragments of the roll on the fire, he threw there, in symbol, his royal house, his doomed city, the temple, and all the people of the land." [1]

At first, indeed, the great king sent only his captains and bands of paid soldiers (2 Kings xxiv. 2) to subdue the distant province. But

[1] *Speaker's Commentary,* v. 315.

when Phoenicia joined in the revolt, Nebuchadnezzar took the field in person.

The object of his earliest attack was Tyre, but finding that he could not take it by assault, he left a part of his army before it and turned to Jerusalem.   That city made no long resistance, and Jehoiakim met his death in the tumult of its capture, being, says Josephus, "thrown before the walls without any burial" (X. vi. 3).

" *They shall not lament for him, saying, Ah my brother! or, Ah sister! they shall not lament for him, saying, Ah lord! or, Ah his glory!* " so ran the words of Jeremiah.   " *He shall be buried with the burial of an ass, drawn and cast forth beyond the gates of Jerusalem.*" [1]

And *Jehoiachin his son reigned in his stead.* But not for long.   " A terror seized on the king of Babylon who had given the kingdom to

---

[1] Jeremiah xxii. 18, 19 ; xxxvi. 30. If these verses refer to the actual death of Jehoiakim (which is not clear), then Josiah was the last king of Jerusalem who was honourably buried in the *sepulchres of his fathers* (2 Chron. xxxv. 24).

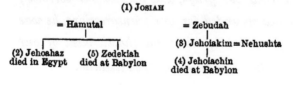

<pre>
                        (1) JOSIAH

            = Hamutal   = Zebudah
               | |
       ┌───────┴───────┐   (3) Jehoiakim = Nehushta
                                            |
   (2) Jehoahaz   (5) Zedekiah   (4) Jehoiachin
   died in Egypt   died at Babylon   died at Babylon
</pre>

Jehoiachin, and that immediately," says Josephus ; " he was afraid that Jehoiachin should bear him a grudge, because of his killing his father, and thereupon should make the country revolt from him " (X. vii. 1). Three months afterwards, therefore, Nebuchadnezzar carried off to Babylon the puppet whom he had made king, together with the queen-mother Nehushta, *all Jerusalem, and the mighty of the land, all the mighty men of valour, . . . and all the craftsmen and smiths : none remained, save the poorest sort of the people of the land* (2 Kings xxiv.).

Jeremiah then, as later by his own choice, stayed with the remnant of the people. He chose to suffer with the most suffering, and in him they saw exemplified the martyr who for the transgression of the people was stricken, who *poured out his soul unto death and bare the sin of many.* It may easily be, as Bunsen was the first to suggest,[1] that it was Jeremiah who was in the mind of the later prophet, when he cried, " *Surely he hath borne our griefs, and carried our sorrows; . . . he was wounded for our transgressions, he was bruised for our iniquities: the chastisement of our*

[1] *Dieu dans l'Histoire*, 31, on Isaiah liii.

*peace was upon him; and with his stripes we are
healed."*

Ezekiel, the young disciple of Jeremiah, was
carried away: and now the depopulation, which
had begun with the first taking of the hostages
seven years before, seemed all but complete; the
Jews who were left behind in their native country
were but *a taunt and a curse.*

For a time Zedekiah, the new king whom
Nebuchadnezzar had set up, was faithful to the
pledge which he had given to the conqueror, *who
had made him swear by God, and to whom he had
given his hand.* For a time he was content that
his kingdom should be a trailing *vine*,[1] living in
the shadow of the great-winged eagle of Babylon.
But soon the old temptation came upon him and
upon his people. Necho of Egypt had been dead
for several years; and now the news came that
his grandson, the young and enterprising Pharaoh
Hophra (or Apries)—he who was, according to
Herodotus, "the most prosperous of all the kings
that ever ruled over Egypt,"—was ready to contest
Babylonian supremacy.

---

[1] Ezek. xvii. The vine was the emblem of the nation.
Stanley, *Sinai and Palestine*, 164.

Zedekiah sent *his ambassadors into Egypt, that they might give him horses and much people.* *"Know ye not what these things mean?"* cried Ezekiel, from his exile by the river Chebar. *"Shall he prosper? Shall he escape that doeth such things?"* (Ezek. xvii.). In vain did Jeremiah exhort the king to put down the idolatry in his own dominions, and to keep his faith with the conqueror. King and priests and people *transgressed very much after all the abominations of the heathen* (2 Chron. xxxvi. 14). *They mocked the messengers of God, and despised his words, and misused his prophets.* In vain did Jeremiah warn them, *rising early and saying,* *"Oh, do not this abominable thing that I hate"* (Jer. xliv. 4). *"Bring your necks under the yoke of the king of Babylon, and serve him,"* was his reiterated message; *"serve him and his people, and live. . . . Hearken not unto the words of the prophets that speak unto you, saying, Ye shall not serve the king of Babylon; for they prophesy a lie unto you"* (xxvii. 12-14).

But the *noise of the stamping of the hoofs of* the Pharaoh's *strong horses, the rushing of his chariots, and the rumbling of his wheels* filled their ears (Jer. xlvii. 3). They chose to believe the words of Hananiah when he told them that the yoke of the king of Babylon was broken, and that in two years the captives would be brought again to Jerusalem. And Jeremiah could only answer sadly, "*Amen : the Lord do so*" (xxviii. 6). "*A wonderful and horrible thing is committed in the land,*" he cried out in his despair; "*the prophets prophesy falsely, and the priests bear rule by their means ; and my people love to have it so : and what will ye do in the end thereof ?*" (v. 30, 31).

The end soon came.

As usual, *the great dragon that lieth in the midst of his rivers* (Ezek. xxix. 3), Egypt, whose *strength is to sit still* (Is. xxx. 7), was slow to move ; and the long-winged Eagle had swooped down upon Jerusalem before Pharaoh Hophra was in the field.

A terrible siege began. One transient gleam of hope shone out when, the Egyptians at last advancing, Nebuchadnezzar raised the siege, and went forth to meet them. But ever there came the warning voice of Jeremiah, saying, "*Behold, Pharaoh's army, which is come forth to help you, shall return to Egypt into their own land. And*

R

the Chaldeans shall come again, and fight against this city, and take it, and burn it with fire. Thus saith the Lord, Deceive not yourselves, saying, The Chaldeans shall surely depart from us: for they shall not depart" (Jer. xxxvii. 7-9).

The Egyptians (whether defeated or no we do not learn) returned to their own land; and then Jerusalem was doomed. For eighteen months longer she held out, until *famine prevailed in the city.* Of the bitter pangs which her children had to bear we read in Lamentations and Ezekiel, as well as in Deuteronomy.[1] The complexions of the men grew black with famine (Lam. iv. 8, v. 10); their skin was withered and parched (iv. 8). Water was scarce as well as food, and could only be *drunken for money* (v. 4). *The tender and delicate woman, which would not adventure to set the sole of her foot upon the ground for delicateness and tenderness* (Deut. xxviii. 56)— she that was *brought up in scarlet*—now *embraced dunghills* in the despairing search for food. *Young children* asked for *bread, and no man*

---

[1] See especially Deut. xxviii. 49-68. The whole work was, thinks M. Renan, composed "du temps de Jérémie, dans l'entourage de Jérémie, d'après les idées de Jérémie" (*Hist.* iii. 236).

broke it unto them (Lam. iv. 4) ; nay, the hands of pitiful women had *sodden their own children. Every sickness and every plague* visited the devoted city. " *They that be slain with the sword are better than they that be slain with hunger,*" said the prophet. *In the morning* men said, *Would God it were even! and at even, Would God it were morning!* because of their ever-present misery and terror (Deut. xxviii. 67).

At length, in the month of July 587, *the famine prevailed in the city, and there was no bread for the people of the land. And the city was broken up* (2 Kings xxv. 3). Zedekiah attempted to escape by flight ; but *the army of the Chaldees pursued after the king, and overtook him in the plains of Jericho : and all his army were scattered from him. So they took the king, and brought him up to the king of Babylon to Riblah ; and they gave judgment upon him. And they slew the sons of Zedekiah before his eyes, and put out the eyes of Zedekiah, and bound him with fetters of brass, and carried him to Babylon* [1]—a bereaved and sightless captive.

---

[1] 2 Kings xxv. "Yet shall he not see it, though he shall die there," Ezekiel (xii. 13) had said ; and Josephus suggests that

" How doth the city sit solitary, that was full of people !
How is she become as a widow ! she that was great among
the nations, and princess among the provinces, how is she
become tributary ! . . . Judah is gone into captivity
. . . she dwelleth among the heathen, she findeth no
rest. . . . Her adversaries are the chief, her enemies
prosper ; for the Lord hath afflicted her for the multitude
of her transgressions : her children are gone into captivity
before the enemy. . . . The adversary hath spread out his
hand upon all her pleasant things : for she hath seen
that the heathen entered into her sanctuary. . . .

" Is it nothing to you, all ye that pass by ? behold, and
see if there be any sorrow like unto my sorrow, which is
done unto me, wherewith the Lord hath afflicted me in
the day of his fierce anger " (Lam. i. 1-12).

*The king of the Chaldees . . . had no compassion
upon young man or maiden, old man, or him that
stooped for age. . . . And all the vessels of the house
of God, great and small, and the treasures of the
house of the Lord, and the treasures of the king, and
of his princes ; all these he brought to Babylon.*
Even Jachin and Boaz, the beautiful pillars
which Solomon had reared up, *did the Chaldees
break in pieces, and carried the brass of them to
Babylon* (2 Kings xxv. 13). *And they burnt the
house of God, and brake down the wall of Jeru-*

this seeming contradiction misled Zedekiah into disbelieving
the prophetic warnings (x. 7, 2 ; viii. 2).

*salem, and burnt all the palaces thereof with fire,
and destroyed all the goodly vessels thereof. And
them that had escaped from the sword carried he
away to Babylon; where they were servants to him
and his sons until the reign of the kingdom of
Persia* (2 Chron. xxxvi. 17-20).

The disastrous news was brought to Ezekiel,
far away on the banks of the Chebar.[1] "*And it
came to pass in the twelfth year of our captivity,*"[2]
he says, "*in the tenth month, in the fifth day of the
month, that one that had escaped out of Jerusalem
came unto me, saying, The city is smitten*" (Ezek.
xxxiii. 21).

So Judah was carried away out of their land
(2 Kings xxv. 21). Again, only the very poorest
were left *to be vine-dressers and husbandmen*
under the wise rulership of Gedaliah; but, after
his murder, even that miserable *remnant of Judah,
that were returned from all nations whither they*

---

[1] The Chebar is believed by some people to have been the
Khabour, one of the branches of the Euphrates, to the banks
of which also the earlier exiles from Samaria had been transported.—Layard, *Nineveh and Babylon*, 283 ; Renan, *Hist. du
Peup.* ii. 535.

[2] That is reckoning from the captivity of Jehoiachin in 598
B.C. But the Israelitish Captivity may be said to have begun
with the taking of the first hostages in 605 B.C.

had been driven, took alarm and fled away into Egypt, carrying Jeremiah the prophet with them (Jer. xliii.).

Very unwillingly Jeremiah went; earnestly he exhorted the remnant to *abide in the land*. " *It shall come to pass*," he warned the people, "*that the sword, which ye feared, shall overtake you there in the land of Egypt, and the famine, whereof ye were afraid, shall follow close after you there in Egypt; and there ye shall die*." " *O ye remnant of Judah, go ye not into Egypt*," he cried (xlii.). But they *obeyed not the voice of the Lord to dwell in the land of Judah. . . . So they came into the land of Egypt . . . thus came they even to Tahpanhes* (xliii.).

At Tahpanhes, or Daphnae, Pharaoh Hophra placed a palace at the disposal of the fugitive princesses, the daughters of Zedekiah (Jer. xliii. 6); and there, standing upon the brickwork pavement or square, *which is at the entry of Pharaoh's house in Tahpanhes*, Jeremiah delivered his prophecy: " *Behold, I will send and take Nebuchadrezzar the king of Babylon, my servant, and will set his throne upon these stones that I have hid; and he shall spread his royal pavilion over them*" (xliii. 10).

Hophra's palace has been discovered by Mr.

Petrie; at the entry of it there is a brickwork platform, and the mound under which it was buried still goes among the Arabs of the neighbourhood by the name of El Kasr el Bint el Yahûdî—the Castle of the Jew's daughter.[1]

To return to the main body of the Jews, those who were carried away to Babylonia with Zedekiah. Crossing the Euphrates by one of its many fords—perhaps at Thapsacus or Tiphsah, the Passage, where Xenophon crossed with the Ten Thousand—they came gradually, through the dwindling hills, to Hit, above Babylon, where begins the dead level plain which was to be the land of their captivity. It was a land of many waters; but the Jews wept as they remembered *the hill of the Lord.*

"*By the waters of Babylon we sat down and wept : when we remembered Thee, O Zion. As for our harps, we hanged them up : upon the trees that are*

---

[1] Miss Edwards, *Pharaoh's Fellahs and Explorers,* 63-69. The word brick-kiln of Jer. xliii. 9 is translated brickwork in the Revised Version, with the alternative reading "pavement" or "square." Such a brickwork platform, open to the air, is called by the Arabs Balât. The *Rahab* of Isaiah li. etc. is an allusion to Hophra's title Ra-haa-ab. Ottley's *Modern Egypt,* 37.

therein. For they that led us away captive required of us there a song, and melody in our heaviness : Sing us one of the songs of Zion.

" How shall we sing the Lord's song : in a strange land ? If I forget thee, O Jerusalem, let my right hand forget her cunning. If I do not remember thee, let my tongue cleave to the roof of my mouth." [1]

Daniel, and the other hostages who had been taken from the royal family and from the families of the Jewish nobles, had met with gentle treatment enough. Eastern monarchs have always taken pride in the beauty and comeliness of their attendants ; and the young Hebrew hostages were delicately nourished in the royal palace. They had indeed to refuse the rich dishes and strong wines in which the luxurious Babylonians delighted, and part of which they were wont to offer to their gods at every meal. To the Jews, not the least bitter part of exile and captivity lay in the pollution of their souls, from being forced to *eat their defiled bread among the Gentiles*

---

[1] Ps. cxxxvii. (Prayer Book). Ewald assigns the following Psalms to the period of the Assyrian captivity:—Ps. 42, 43, 83, 17, 16, 49, 22, 25, 38, 88, 14, 120, 121, 123, 130, 131. "Ps. 42, 43, 83, are," he says, "of special interest, as they were probably composed by King Jehoiachin."—*Hist.* iv. 269.

(Ezek. iv. 13). It was a *sacrifice to devils*; and St. Paul gave literal expression to the Jewish feeling when he said, *Ye cannot drink the cup of the Lord and the cup of devils* (1 Cor. x. 21). But when it was found that the young Hebrews at the Babylonian court throve equally well on their chosen diet of " pulse " (dried dates pressed into cakes, gourds, melons and cucumbers), they were allowed to have their way in this matter.

They were taught " *the learning and the tongue of the Chaldeans,*" that is to say, the ancient Accadian language, which was, like Latin in the middle ages, the language of devotion and of literature. Like the "muttering monks" of old, with their

> " Bells and books and mysteries,"

the Chaldeans were the scientific body, the statesmen and priest-magicians of their day ; the vast and lofty temple of Belus serving them "at once as a place of worship and an astronomical observatory." [1]

"Here," says Diodorus, in his account of 'the things done in Asia in antient times,' "it will not be amiss to say something of the Chaldeans (as

---

[1] Grote, *Hist.* iii. 391.

the Babylonians call them) and of their antiquity,
that nothing worth remark may be omitted.
They, being the most ancient Babylonians, hold
the same station and dignity in the commonwealth
as the Egyptian priests do in Egypt ; for being
deputed to divine offices, they spend all their time
in the study of philosophy, and are especially
famous for the art of astrology.   They are mightily
given to divination, and foretell future events, and
employ themselves either by purifications, sacrifices, or other enchantments to avert evils or pro-
cure good fortune and success."   This knowledge,
he adds, they learn " by tradition from their
ancestors, the son from the father " (ii. 3).

Their learning was no doubt mixed with much
pretence and imposture.   They were too much
advanced in science to believe in the magic arts
which they professed to practise.   But it has truly
been said that there were few of the paths of knowledge in which they had not taken at least the
first step.

They had made a chart of the heavens, had
calculated the eclipses, had observed the courses
of the planets, or wanderers ; had invented sun-
dials, and water-clocks, and magnifying-glasses.

The inscriptions on their tablets deal with almost every branch of knowledge; and they had, as we have seen, kept an exact record of the movements of all the heavenly bodies since the year 2234 B.C.

Among these wise men Daniel grew up and learnt *wisdom and understanding*—then, as throughout his life, faithfully serving his Babylonian master.

Meanwhile the great mass of the captives, those who were not singled out to *stand before the king*, were told off to work at the repairs of the huge temple of Belus, or at the vast reservoirs and canals —the *waters of Babylon* which Nebuchadnezzar seems to have regarded as his most important works.

"Against presumptuous enemies, who were hostile to the men of Babylon, great waters like the waters of the ocean I made use of abundantly. Their depths were like the depths of the vast ocean. I did not allow the waters to overflow, but the fulness of their floods I caused to flow on, restraining them with a brick embankment. . . . Thus I completely made strong the defences of Babylon. May it last for ever!"[1]

---

[1] Standard inscription of Nebuchadnezzar, Rawlinson's *Herodotus*, iii. 587. See *Rec.* v. 119, 135.

Nebuchadnezzar, meanwhile, went on with his conquests. In 573 B.C. he brought to an end the long siege of Tyre, that proud Phoenician city, which had felt no sympathy with her sister Jerusalem, but had triumphed at her fall, saying, "*Aha, she is broken that was the gates of the people. . . . I shall be replenished, now she is laid waste*" (Ezek. xxvi. 2). "For the last time, through the piercing eyes of Ezekiel, we see the Queen of ancient commerce in all her glory, under the figure of one of her own stately vessels, sailing proudly over her subject seas, with the fine linen of Egypt for her white sails, with the purple from the isles of Greece for the drapery of her seats, with merchant princes for her pilots and her mariners." [1]

Six years later (567 B.C.) Nebuchadnezzar marched into Egypt, plundered her of all her treasures, and deposed Hophra (the last of the Pharaohs), a general named Amasis being installed upon the throne in his stead, as a vassal of Babylonia.

It may have been on his return from one of those expeditions, when his treasury would be

[1] Stanley, *Jewish Church*, ii. 572.

overflowing with the plunder of Egypt and of
Tyre, that *Nebuchadnezzar the king made an image
of gold* and *set it up in the plain of Dura in the province of Babylon,* commanding that at the sound of
music all *people, nations, and languages,* should fall
down and worship it.   No doubt the image represented the great Babylonian deity, Bel Marduk, "of
lordship and dominion," the patron of the king.   It
was the sign and symbol that "the great autocrat
would own no lord on earth above himself, and no
God in heaven save the one whom he had chosen
to be his." [1]   It is probable that no thought of
proselytism was in the king's mind : he merely
wished for outward submission—absolute and un-
questioning—to the god of his royal choice.[2]

It was given to the Three Holy Children to
remain steadfast in a nobler faith.   Such an
action as theirs was, no doubt, in the mind of the
second Isaiah, when, then or later in the captivity,
he wrote that scathing denunciation of the folly
of idol-worshippers.   "*They lavish gold out of the
bag, and weigh silver in the balance, and hire a*

---

[1] Hunter, *Story of Daniel,* 126.   See *Rec.* N. S. iv. 108.
[2] "The tendency of barbarous theology is to retain the
exclusive favour of their gods.   Proselytism has no part in it."
—Sir J. Lubbock, *Essays,* 196.

goldsmith ; and he maketh it a god : they fall down, yea, they worship. They bear him upon the shoulder, they carry him, and set him in his place, and he standeth ; from his place shall he not remove : yea, one shall cry unto him, yet can he not answer, nor save him out of his trouble. Remember this," the prophet cried, *"and shew yourselves men."* [1] The three Hebrews remembered it, and they made answer like men to King Nebuchadnezzar *in his rage and fury. " If it be so, our God, whom we serve, is able to deliver us from the burning fiery furnace, and he will deliver us out of thine hand, O king. But if not, be it known unto thee, O king, that we will not serve thy gods, nor worship the golden image which thou hast set up."* [2] Ultimately, so runs the story, Nebuchadnezzar recognised the

---

[1] Isaiah xlvi. 6-8 ; see also xliv. 16. "For health he calleth upon that which is weak ; for life, prayeth to that which is dead ; for aid, humbly beseecheth that which hath least means to help ; and for a good journey he asketh of that which cannot set a foot forward."—Wisdom of Solomon, xiii. 18.

[2] Dan. iii. 17. These were the words which Samuel Wesley (the father of John and Charles) took as his text on that famous Sunday, when, instead of reading James II.'s Declaration of Indulgence, "as he was required, and although surrounded with courtiers, soldiers, and informers, he preached boldly against the designs of the court."—Southey, *Life of Wesley,* 10, ed. 1864.

power of the God of the Hebrews, and proceeded to do haughty homage to the foreign deity
by decreeing *that every people, nation, and language,*
which speak any thing amiss against the God of
Shadrach, Meshach, and Abednego, shall be cut in
pieces, and their houses shall be made a dunghill.

All people, nations, and languages of the
then known world were indeed, in very truth,
subject to Nebuchadnezzar's decree. For thirty-
three years he had pursued his conquests, and now
he could remain *at rest in his house and flourishing*
in his palace (Dan. iv. 4). From Persia in the
east to Libya in the west, from Cilicia in the north
to Arabia in the south, he was lord and master
of all; and he now proceeded to use his boundless
power for the building and beautifying of the
golden city, which was the pride and joy of his
life.

Whole nations laboured in his service; from
the ancient capitals of Egypt, from the hills and
valleys of Syria, from the merchant cities of
Phoenicia, the *net* of the conqueror was spread
wide over all. He gathered them in his drag,
and *rejoiced* and was *glad.* " *Therefore,*" said the
prophet, " *they sacrifice unto their net, and burn*

incense unto their drag."[1] All men alike, from far or near, friends or foes, met in common humiliation beneath the walls of his cities. With his "unbounded command of naked human strength"[2] Nebuchadnezzar could, and did, build a city which was the "wonder of mankind." But for him Babylon would have had little place in history : hardly any other name than his is found upon her bricks. The ancient city, as he left it, had become his creation, a mighty monument to his boundless power.

Her empire, which lasted at most for eighty-eight years, was for nearly half the time under his sway. Babylon has almost more entirely disappeared than any other of the great towns of antiquity : *a drought is upon her waters* (Jer. l. 38); her well-ordered canals are *a possession for the bittern* (Is. xiv. 23), the *wild beasts of the desert cry* in her *desolate houses* and in her *pleasant palaces* (Is. xiii. 21, 22). Palaces and temples, *swept with the besom of destruction* (Is. xiv. 23), are now but shapeless mounds of sandy earth; yet "to this day there are men who have no

[1] Hab. i. 15. See also Ezek. xii. 13, xvii. 20, xxxii. 3.
[2] Grote, *Hist.* iii. 405, ed. 1851.

other trade than that of gathering bricks from this
vast heap and taking them for sale to the neighbouring towns and villages; . . . and as the
traveller passes through the narrow streets, he

VIEW OF BABIL FROM THE WEST.—After Rawlinson (Murray).

sees in the walls of every hovel a record of the
glory and power of Nebuchadnezzar." To this
day may be found, among the rubbish, fragments
of brick which are as brilliantly coloured as when
they were turned out from the hands of Nebuchadnezzar's workmen. The chief colours are " a

s

brilliant blue, red, a deep yellow, white and black. We learn from ancient authors that the walls of the palaces of Babylon were painted with the figures of men and animals, and there can be no doubt that these enamelled bricks are from the walls of an edifice."[1] "And," says Diodorus, "whereas the Euphrates runs through the middle of Babylon, making its course to the south, the palaces lie the one on the east, and the other on the west side of the river; both built at exceeding costs and expense. For that on the west had an high and stately wall, made of well-burnt bricks, sixty furlongs in compass; within this was drawn another of a round circumference, upon which were pourtrayed in the bricks before they were burnt all sorts of living creatures, as if it were to the life, laid with great art in curious colours . . . artificially expressed, in most lively colours " (ii. 1).

All this helps us to reconstruct in our minds the golden city, with its massive temples and palaces, standing high on their brickwork platforms and blazing with colour in the sunshine; with its

---

[1] Layard, *Nineveh and Babylon*, 506, 507. See the "*men pourtrayed upon the wall, the images of the Chaldeans pourtrayed with vermilion* " of Ezekiel (xxiii. 14).

wonderful hanging gardens—the "meadows on
mountain tops" which Nebuchadnezzar had raised
up to remind his queen, Amytis, of the wind-swept
rocky terraces of Ecbatana, her far-off Median
home.[1]

Babylon was, says Herodotus (i. 178), "adorned
in a manner surpassing any city we are acquainted
with." But it is her vast size which seems
most to have struck all ancient observers. The
huge four-square city is said to have covered a
space five times as large as London is now; but
it was in truth not so much a city as "an
embattled district," whose huge walls encircled
parks and pleasure-grounds and fields, as well as
massive temples and gorgeous palaces. Within
an inner rampart rose on one side the temple of
Belus, on the other the royal palace and treasure-
house of the king. All the space between the
two walls was filled with gardens, following "the
silvery lines of the canals," or with fields of
waving corn and maize, and millet and sesame,
growing so luxuriantly that Herodotus declared

[1] See Berosus, Cory's *Fragments*, 39 ; *Diodorus* (Booth), ii. 1.
But "Herodotus is in fact our only original witness, speaking
from his own observation, and going into details, respecting the
marvels of Babylon."—Grote, iii. 399 note.

he should not say "to what height they grow,
though within my own knowledge ; for I am
not ignorant that what I have already written
concerning the fruitfulness of Babylonia must
seem incredible to those who have never visited
the country." [1]

Lady of Kingdoms, Babylon "lifted herself
to heaven from broad wharves and ramparts, by
wide flights of stairs and terraces, high walls and
hanging gardens, pyramids and towers,—so colossal
in her buildings, so imperially lavish of space
between." [2]   From corner to corner of this vast
district flowed the river Euphrates, the broad highway of commerce for *the Chaldeans, whose cry is in
the ships* (Is. xliii. 14).   From east to west Babylonian commerce had spread far and wide ; she
had become *a land of traffick,* a *city of merchants*
(Ezek. xvii. 4): her streets were thronged with
merchandise ; her inhabitants exceeded in *dyed*

---

[1] i. 193. The land is now a desert, but this is because ot
the "neglect of the watercourses.   Left to themselves the
rivers tend to desert some portions of the alluvium wholly,
which then become utterly unproductive ; while they spread
themselves out over others, which are converted thereby into
pestilential swamps."—Rawlinson, *Five Great Monarchies,* i. 42.
See also Layard, *Nineveh and Babylon,* 539.

[2] G. Adam Smith, *Isaiah* ii. 55.

attire upon their heads, all of them princes to look to.
Her trade was in *gold, and silver, and precious*
stones, and pearls, and fine linen, and purple, and
silk, and scarlet . . . and horses, and chariots, and
slaves, and souls of men " (Rev. xviii. 12, 13). Her
luxury was equal to her magnificence. Lebanon
furnished her cedars ; Tyre, her goods and merchandise ; Syria, the wines and fruits which
loaded the tables of her princes. The imagery
of the traffic on the Euphrates was so deeply
engrained in the minds of the Jewish people, that
they applied it to the inland capital on the banks
of the narrow Tiber; and six centuries after the
time of the second Isaiah the words *Babylon is*
fallen came to the lips of " another Jewish exile,
who, on the rock of Patmos, heard and repeated
again with the same thrill of exultation, ' *Babylon*
the great is fallen, is fallen.' " [1] Thus, overthrown
in Genesis, cursed in Revelation, Babylon is, from
end to end of the Bible, the very type and symbol
of all that is corrupt and unholy.

This power and glory, this pomp and luxury,
were the creation of King Nebuchadnezzar ; and,
recorded on many a cylinder now placed in the

[1] Stanley, *Jewish Church*, iii. 64.

INSCRIPTION ON A BRONZE STEP OF NEBUCHADNEZZAR.

1.

D.P. Na - bi - um - ku - du - ur - ri - u - ṣu - ur

Nebuchadnezzar

sar   ka - dingi - ra - ki

the king of Babylon (the gate of god)

2.

za - ni - in   E   SAG - ILI   u   E   ZI - DA

the restorer of the temple Sagili and the temple Zida

3.

ablu   asaridu   sa   D.P.   Nabu - abla

the   eldest   son   of   Nabu - pal-

u - ṣu - ur   sar   tin - tir - ki   a - na - ku

uṣur the king of Babylon (the seat of life) am I.

4.

a - na   D.P.   Na - bi - um   bil - ni   ṣi - i - ri

For   the   god   Nabo,   the   supreme   lord

5.

mu - sa - ri - ku - u - um   ma - la - ki - ya

the lengthener of the day of my rule (or kingdom)

6.

E - ZI - DA   bit - su   i - na   Bar - si - pa ki

E-Zida   his temple   in   Borsippa

es - si - is   e - pu - us

afresh   I built (made)

British Museum, we see his pride and pleasure in that " Babylon which is the delight of my eyes and which I have glorified." "The temple of Zida I built anew. With silver and gold and precious stones, *mesukan* wood and cedar, I completed its roof. The temple of the planet, which is the tower of Babylon, I built and I finished it." "O Sun! great Lord! when thou shalt enter in joy and gladness into the temple of Tara, thy divine dwelling-place, regard with pleasure the pious works of my hands! And a life of prolonged days, a firm throne, a long reign, may thy lips proclaim for me " (*Rec.* vii. 72).

In the book of Daniel we read that as *he walked in the palace of the kingdom of Babylon, the king spake and said, Is not this great Babylon, that I have built for the house of the kingdom by the might of my power, and for the honour of my majesty?* (Dan. iv. 29).[1] It was *while the word was in the king's mouth* that there came upon him that terrible and hideous form of madness known as Lycanthropy, which changes a *man's heart* into a *beast's* (iv. 16) and *drives him* from among his kind.[2]

---

[1] Cf. *Rec.* v. 119-135.

[2] The history of this time was written four centuries later

It is not surprising that Berosus should leave the story of this time untold, and that no express mention of it is to be found among these cylinders on which the great king recorded for all time the might of his majesty and power. But there is in the standard inscription of Nebuchadnezzar a passage (very difficult of translation by reason of its " studied ambiguity " of phrase) in which the king appears to say—" For four years (?) . . . the seat of my kingdom in the city . . . did not rejoice my heart. In all my dominions I did not build a high place of power; the precious treasures of my kingdom I did not lay up. In Babylon, buildings for myself and the honour of my kingdom I did

by a Hebrew writer, who thought that if he put before his countrymen the story of Daniel's life, and of the great over- throw of Babylon by Cyrus, it would give them courage to resist the cruel Syrian conqueror Antiochus Epiphanes. The suffer- ing Hebrews of that day (170 B.C.) were to be cheered and comforted by reading of the overthrow of former tyrants, as powerful and as pitiless as their own enemy. " It was at this crisis, in the sultry heat of an age thus frightfully oppressive, that this book appeared with its sword-edge utterance, its piercing exhortation to endure in face of the despot, and its promise, full of divine joy, of near and sure salvation " (*Ewald*, v. 303; Stanley, *Jewish Church*, iii. 301). The touches of description in the book of Daniel are yearly receiving con- firmation from the cylinders discovered and interpreted by Chaldean scholars.

not lay out. In the worship of Merodach my lord, the joy of my heart, in Babylon, the city of his sovereignty and the seat of my empire, I did not sing his praises, and I did not furnish his altars, nor did I clear out his canals." [1]

In the book of Daniel we read that, unable to bear the sight of the palaces and temples he had *builded with blood* (Hab. ii. 12), the mighty monarch wandered for years in the fields, *and did eat grass as oxen, and his body was wet with the dew of heaven, till his hairs were grown like eagles' feathers, and his nails like birds' claws* (Dan. iv. 33). When his *understanding returned unto him*, he is represented as declaring, "*Now I Nebuchadnezzar praise and extol and honour the King of heaven*"—possibly the "*God of Daniel*," again exalted for a time to an equal rank with Marduk, "Lord of lords" (*Rec.* vii. 71), or with "Nebo, who bestows the thrones of heaven and earth" (vii. 75). For the religion of Nebuchadnezzar was that of Ur-Bau and Dungi, alike in the objects and the mode of worship; and though different gods were at different times exalted to the highest rank, the deities on the whole remained the same.

---

[1] Rawlinson, *Herodotus*, iii. 586.

Nebuchadnezzar seems to have reigned for a few years after his restoration to health; but his dynasty did not long survive him. His son, Amil-Marduk, the Evil-Merodach of the Bible, was driven from the throne by a plot among the nobles —some say because of the favour which he showed to the Jewish captive king, in that he *did lift up the head of Jehoiachin king of Judah out of prison; and spake kindly to him, and set his throne above the throne of the kings that were with him in Babylon.*[1]

"In the later traditions of his countrymen this story of the comparative ease of the last representative of David was yet further enlarged with the tale how he sat with his fellow-exiles on the banks of the Euphrates and listened to Baruch, who had himself meanwhile been transported hither from Egypt; or how that he married a beautiful countrywoman of the name of Susanna,"[2] and lived in comfort, with a "fair garden joining unto his house" (Susannah i. 4).

Evil-Merodach was succeeded by Neriglissar,

---

[1] 2 Kings xxv. 27, 28. See also Josephus, *Ant. Jud.* x. 11, 2.

[2] Stanley, *Jewish Church*, iii. 22, quoting Baruch i. 3, and Josephus, *Ant.* x. 9, 7.

whose title upon his bricks is Rubû-êmgu, and who is perhaps identical with the "Nergal-shareser, Rab-mag," who was one of the *king of Babylon's princes* before Jerusalem (Jer. xxxix. 13).

After some years of short and troubled reigns the throne was usurped by a noble called Nabonidus (555 B.C.), who married the daughter of Nebuchadnezzar, and whose son (associated with him in the sovereignty) was the Belshazzar of Daniel V.[1]

---

[1] Belshazzar is said not to have been more than fourteen years old at the time; but Eastern children are often thus precocious. Layard (*Nineveh and Babylon*, 487) describes his doing business at Hillah with the twelve-year-old son of the aged governor. "It was with this child that, in common with the inhabitants of Hillah, I transacted business. He received and paid visits with wonderful dignity and decorum. His notes and his inquiries after my health and wants were couched in the most eloquent and suitable terms. . . . On the whole he made as good and active a governor as I have often met with in an Eastern town." On the cylinders of Nabonidus found by Sir H. Rawlinson at Mugheir (Ur), the protection of the gods is asked for Nabu-nahid and his son Bel-shar-usur, who are coupled together in a manner that implies joint sovereignty. We are reminded that the "Belshazzar the king" of Daniel V. could only offer to whomsoever should relieve his overpowering terror that he should be "*third ruler in the kingdom.*"

609. Battle of Megiddo.   Josiah slain.
606. Necho defeated at Carchemish by Nebuchadnezzar.
599. Jerusalem captured.   Jehoiachin sent to Babylon.
588. Destruction of Jerusalem.   Zedekiah captured.   Gedaliah slain.
567. Hophra dethroned in Egypt.   Amasis established.
561. Nebuchadnezzar dies.   Evil-Merodach king.
559. Nergal-shareser king.
560. Cyrus king of Elam.
555. Nabonidus king of Babylon.
549. Cyrus of Elam conquers Astyages of Media.
538. Babylon captured by Cyrus.

CHAPTER VI

"A sound of a cry cometh from Babylon, and great destruction from the land of the Chaldeans: Because the Lord hath spoiled Babylon, and destroyed out of her the great voice; when her waves do roar like great waters, a noise of their voice is uttered: Because the spoiler is come upon her, even upon Babylon, and her mighty men are taken, every one of their bows is broken: for the Lord God of recompences shall surely requite. And I will make drunk her princes, and her wise men, her captains, and her rulers, and her mighty men: and they shall sleep a perpetual sleep, and not wake, saith the King, whose name is The Lord of hosts. Thus saith the Lord of hosts, The broad walls of Babylon shall be utterly broken, and her high gates shall be burned with fire; and the people shall labour in vain."—Jer. li. 54-58.

"Thou shalt take up this proverb against the king of Babylon, and say, How hath the oppressor ceased! the golden city ceased!"
—Is. xiv. 4.

"At the noise of the taking of Babylon the earth is moved, and the cry is heard among the nations."—Jer. l. 46.

"A sword is upon their horses, and upon their chariots, and upon all the mingled people that are in the midst of her; . . . a sword is upon her treasures."—Jer. l. 37.

MEANWHILE, a new power was rising up in the East. Cyrus of Persia, the young *"prince and*

commander" (Is. lv. 4), the "*eagle*" (xlvi. 11), the
"*righteous man from the east*" (xli. 2), who was to
make so great a mark in the history of the world,
had begun his career of conquest. *Kings,* we
read, were given *as the dust to his sword, and as
driven stubble to his bow* (Is. xli. 2).

The year of his accession (560 B.C.) is, says
Dean Stanley, a "great date" in ancient history.[1]
Not only was it the date of the accession to power
of Cyrus in Persia, but that also of Croesus in
Lydia, and of Peisistratus in Athens; while, in
566, Amasis had been set upon the throne of
Egypt, and in 572 Tarquinius Superbus had
succeeded to that of Rome. Before this time we
have, "properly speaking, no history"—no con-
tinuous chronicle—of any nation, with the single
exception of the Israelites. "But with the appearance of the Persians," says a brilliant French
writer, "the movement of history begins, and

---

[1] "Many of us," says Matthew Arnold, "have a kind of centre
point in the far past to which we make things converge, from
which our thoughts of history instinctively start and to which
they return. . . . Our education is such that we are strongly
led to take this centre point in the history of Greece or Rome ;
but it may be doubted whether one who took the conquest of
Babylon and the restoration of the Jewish exiles would not
have a better."—*Great Prophecy,* xxxv.

Humanity throws itself into that restless march
of progress which henceforth is never to cease." [1]
With Peisistratus and Croesus begins our definite
knowledge of Greece ; with them began that
noble series of statesmen and soldiers and writers
—writers " whose career had run parallel to the
tragedy of actual life "—who made her literature
and her history.

And not only was Daniel the contemporary of
Peisistratus and Croesus, of Solon and of Thales ;
but Cyrus, the hero and the deliverer of the
captive Jews, was the hero and the pattern of the
conquering Greeks.

He had ascended the throne of Persia in the
year after the death of Nebuchadnezzar, and already the *" righteous man from the east"* was
coming *"from the north,"* [2] for Media had been
absorbed in his dominions, and the Greek cities
of Asia Minor were beginning to feel his power.
Croesus of Lydia had taken alarm, and in the very
year in which Nabonidus became king of Babylon,
there arrived ambassadors from Sardis to suggest

---

[1] Stanley, *Jewish Church*, iii. 51 ; quoting Quinet, *Génie des
Religions*, 301, 302.

[2] Is. xli. 2, 25 ; Ezek. xxvi. 7.

a league against the common foe. This suggestion
Nabonidus seems to have accepted, and to have begun those great works of defence which Herodotus
ascribes to the Nitocris, of whom he tells us that,
"observing the great power and restless enterprise
of the Medes, who had taken so large a number
of cities, and among them Nineveh, and expecting
to be attacked in her turn, (she) made all possible
exertions to increase the defences of her empire "
(i. 185).

But Nabonidus seems to have been on the
whole of an inert and unwarlike character; and
before his preparations were complete, his ally
Croesus had precipitated the struggle, had seen
his capital razed to the ground, and was himself a
helpless captive in the hands of the great conqueror. Cyrus was thus left without an active
enemy to bar his way.

The captive Jews in Babylon must have heard
of his victories with beating hearts. Many of
them had no doubt followed the advice sent by
Jeremiah from Jerusalem *to all that were carried
away captives into Babylon. Thus saith the Lord
. . . Build ye houses, and dwell in them*, Jeremiah
had written, in that early epistle which · was

perhaps the first example of its kind,[1] *and plant
gardens, and eat the fruit of them ; take ye wives,
and beget sons and daughters . . . And seek the
peace of the city whither I have caused you to be
carried away captives, and pray unto the Lord for
it : for in the peace thereof shall ye have peace.*
Until *seventy years were accomplished*, they were
to serve their Chaldean conqueror—as it were to
render unto Caesar the things that were Caesar's—
even while never losing faith in the "*good word*"
of the Lord, in the promised restoration to their
native land (Jer. xxix.).

Now the seventy years were all but accomplished.   Jerusalem had indeed *received of the
Lord's hand double for all her sins* (Is. xl. 2).
She had been tried *in the furnace of affliction*
(xlviii. 10) ; she had *drunken the dregs of the cup
of trembling and wrung them out* (li. 17); she had
been *tossed with tempest and not comforted* (liv.
11).   No wonder that in the ears of her children
should ring the great prophecy of "Isaiah,"
the good tidings of *liberty to the captives and the
opening of prison to them that are bound*, which
he was preaching to the afflicted.

[1] *Jewish Church*, iii. 17. See also Ewald, v. 10 ; Baruch, i. 2.

T

The Great Unknown prophet of the deliverance[1] had a very different task from the Isaiah of a hundred and fifty years before. He addressed a people living, not upon their own soil, but in exile and servitude, with no responsibilities or power of action, with nothing to sustain them except the message which it was his mission to confirm.

He is unknown to us, Renan has finely said, as the author of the book of Job is unknown, as Homer is unknown, and the author of the *Imitation*. "Sait-on qui a fait Homère, qui a fait l'Imitation de Jésus-Christ ? François de Sales a dit le mot juste sur de tels livres : 'Leur véritable auteur c'est le Saint-Esprit.'"[2] The exact date when he lived—whether his burning words were prophecies uttered long beforehand, or were a record of events which he himself witnessed—may be a

---

[1] It is now generally agreed that chapters xl.-lxvi. of "Isaiah" are not by the same hands as the preceding part of the book, and were written at a much later time. With these twenty-seven chapters many critics class the 13th, parts of the 14th and 21st, the chapters from the 24th to the 27th, and the 34th and 35th. Ewald calls the author of chapters xl.-lxvi "der grosse Ungenannte" (the Great Unnamed), and considers that he probably wrote in Egypt, at an even later time than the authors of the other fragments (*Prophets*, iv. 256).

[2] *Hist. d'Israel*, iii. 503.

matter of conjecture.[1]   In any case "the greatness
of Hebrew prophecy, or even its special character,
are not concerned." "In my belief," says Mr.
Arnold, "the unique grandeur of the Hebrew
prophets consists, indeed, not in the curious fore-
telling of details, but in the unerring vision with
which they saw, the unflinching boldness and
sublime force with which they said, that the great
unrighteous kingdoms of the heathen could not
stand, and that the world's salvation lay in a
recourse to the God of Israel."[2]

"*How hath the oppressor ceased! the golden city
ceased!*" was the proverb which Isaiah had to
take up against the king of Babylon (xiv. 4).
"*Thus saith the Lord to his anointed, to Cyrus,
whose right hand I have holden, to subdue nations
before him; I will ungird the loins of kings, to
open before him the two-leaved gates; and the gates
shall not be shut; I will go before thee, and make*

---

[1] If Is. xli. 25 refers to the absorption of Media (north of
Babylon), then the date of the second Isaiah must be between
549 and 538 B.C., when "Cyrus is on the way of triumph, but
Babylon has still to fall." In any case "there are very few
chapters in the whole of the Old Testament whose date can be
fixed so precisely as the date of chapters xl.-xlviii." (G. A.
Smith, *Isaiah*, 12).

[2] M. Arnold, *Great Prophecy*, xxix.

the crooked places straight : I will break in pieces the gates of brass, and cut in sunder the bars of iron " (xlv. 1-2).

" *Sing, O heavens ; and be joyful, O earth ; and break forth into singing, O mountains : for the Lord hath comforted his people, and will have mercy upon his afflicted* " (xlix. 13).

" *Arise, shine ; for thy light is come, and the glory of the Lord is risen upon thee. . . . And the sons of strangers shall build up thy walls, and their kings shall minister unto thee : for in my wrath I smote thee, but in my favour have I had mercy on thee* " (lx.).

" *My counsel shall stand, and I will do all my pleasure : calling the eagle from the east, the man that executeth my counsel from a far country : yea, I have spoken it, I will also bring it to pass ; I have purposed it, I will also do it* " (xlvi. 10, 11).

" *The redeemed of the Lord shall return, and come with singing unto Zion ; and everlasting joy shall be upon their head : they shall obtain gladness and joy ; and sorrow and mourning shall flee away* " (li. 11).

" *How beautiful upon the mountains are the feet of him that bringeth good tidings, that publisheth peace; . . . that saith unto Zion, Thy God reigneth !"* (lii. 7).

We cannot wonder that the Jews should have looked to Cyrus as their Redeemer, for "it can hardly be without foundation that both in Greek and in Hebrew literature he is represented as the type of a just and gentle prince."[1] His monotheism is a matter of dispute. There is evidence that he entered Babylon as the " servant of Merodach," whose priests Nabonidus had vexed by his neglect. " Merodach, the lord of the gods, grieved," says an inscription. " He sought out a King for himself who would perform according to the heart's desire of the god whatever was entrusted to his hand. He proclaimed the renown of Cyrus, the king of Anzan (Persia)."[2] And, in the historical romance of Xenophon, he is no doubt truly represented as sacrificing to " Vesta and Jupiter the king," and to " whatever other deity the image directed " (vii. 5, 57). It may have been in this politic spirit that he addressed the Jews in the name of the " Lord God of Israel " (Ezra i. 3); but it is very probable that to a certain extent he did

[1] Stanley, *Jewish Church,* iii. 53.
[2] Budge, *Babylonian Life and History,* 79.

identify the Jehovah of the Jews with Ormazd, the one supreme god of the Medo - Persic people.[1]

Undoubtedly the main feature of the Persian religion in his day was "the acknowledgment and the worship of a single supreme God—'the Lord God of Heaven'—'the giver (*i.e.* maker) of heaven and earth'—the disposer of thrones, the dispenser of happinesses. The foremost place in inscriptions and decrees was assigned, almost universally, to the '*great* god Ormazd.' Every king of whom we have an inscription more than two lines in length speaks of Ormazd as his upholder; and the early monarchs mention by name no other god. All rule 'by the grace of Ormazd.' From Ormazd come victory, conquest, safety, prosperity, blessings of every kind. The 'law of Ormazd' is the rule of life."[2]

The Persians "have no images of the gods," Herodotus tells us, "no temples, no altars, and consider the use of them a sign of folly."

Cyrus was the leader of a "valiant-minded

---

[1] Rawlinson, *Historical Ill.* 179, and *Five Great Mon.* ii. 421, 431; Oort's *Bible for Young People*, 129; Renan, *Hist. d'Is.*, iii. 464; Budge, *Babylonian Life*, etc., 87.

[2] Rawlinson, *Five Great Monarchies* (1871), iii. 347.

people," a people who had been taught "three
things : to back a horse, to bend the bow, and to
speak the truth,"—a people as temperate and
just and hardy as the Chaldeans were *delicate* and
corrupt and cruel. He had, withal, the quality of
success. " I have always," Xenophon makes him
say upon his deathbed, to the friends and children
gathered round him, " seemed to feel my strength
increase with the advance of time, so that I have
not found myself weaker in my old age than in
my youth, nor do I know that I have attempted
or desired anything in which I have not been
successful." [1]

But though the Jews might tremble with
excitement at the coming of Cyrus, the Babylonians themselves seem to have felt very little fear.
Even when Croesus of Lydia had been defeated
and Sardis his capital destroyed ; when king

---

[1] *Cyropædia*, viii. 7, 6. In teaching a child the history of this
time, its interest is, however, best awakened by reading it a
Bowdlerized version of the history of Cyrus's earlier years, in
the first book of Herodotus. "The *Cyropædia*, says Cicero,
was written *non ad historiæ fidem, sed effigiem justi imperii*,
not in conformity with the truth of history, but to exhibit
a representation of an excellent government."—J. S. Watson,
Preface, xi. Herodotus is more entertaining, as well as more
instructive.

Nabonidus himself had been beaten and forced to take shelter within the walls of the treasure city Borsippa, leaving Belshazzar to defend Babylon against the Persian host—even then the citizens continued to lead their old life of corrupting luxury. They were safe behind the shelter of those huge walls which Nebuchadnezzar had built with "bricks burnt as hard as stones, in masses like mountains" —the *broad walls of Babylon*, which (according to the measurements given us by Herodotus) were fifteen miles long each way, and which must have been high as the Victoria Tower at Westminster, as broad at the top as a wide street. Within those defences were wide fields, where harvests could ripen and cattle could graze, where husbandmen and vinedressers could labour undisturbed by the warfare without; and in the "king's quarter" of the city were stored corn and wine and oil in plenty. "For," says Herodotus, "as they had been long aware of the restless spirit of Cyrus, and saw that he attacked all nations alike, they had laid up provisions for many years, and therefore were under no apprehensions about a siege."[1]

[1] Herod. I. 190. See also Xenophon, *Cyro.* vii. 5, 13.

"Whether therefore some one else made the suggestion to him in his perplexity, or whether he himself devised the plan, he had recourse to the following stratagem. Having stationed the bulk of his army near the passage of the river where it enters Babylon, and again having stationed another division beyond the city, where the river makes its exit, he gave orders to his forces to enter the city as soon as they should see the stream fordable. Having thus stationed his forces, and given these directions, he himself marched away with the ineffective part of his army " (i. 191).

No doubt the Babylonians, looking down from their ramparts, noticed that a large part of the besieging army had disappeared. Perhaps they thought that Cyrus was giving up the siege in despair, and so grew more and more confident, less and less careful in guarding their gates and river walls. But, meanwhile, the soldiers of the Persian army were secretly busy with a task for which their far-sighted commander had prepared them, in the days when he seemed to be wreaking

"Those who were on the walls laughed at the blockade, as being furnished with provisions for more than twenty years."

the senseless vengeance of a tyrant upon the river Gyndes, wherein one of the white horses of Ormazd had been drowned.[1]

Bow and spear were powerless against the battlements of Babylon: the spade was to be the weapon of Persian attack.   For the plan of Cyrus was to divert the water of the Euphrates into a new channel, and to march his soldiers into the very heart of the city along the thoroughfare thus formed by the ancient river-bed.

Perhaps the Jews within the city apprised him of the great religious feast that was to be held, when all the people of Babylon—nobles and commons alike—would be absorbed in feasting and revelry.[2] Certain it is that on a night of feasting the

---

[1] "When Cyrus reached this stream, which could only be passed in boats, one of the sacred white horses accompanying his march, full of spirit and high mettle, walked into the water, and tried to cross by himself; but the current seized him, swept him along with it, and drowned him in its depths. Cyrus, enraged at the insolence of the river, threatened so to break its strength that in future even women should cross it easily without wetting their knees."—Herodotus, i. 189.

[2] Berosus mentions feast of Sacea, which lasted five days, "in which it is the custom that the masters should obey their domestics, one of whom is led round the house, clothed in royal garment, and him they call Zoganes."—*Cory's Fragments*, 43.

final blow was struck. "The trenches were now dug; and Cyrus, when he heard that there was a festival in Babylon, in which all the Babylonians drank and revelled the whole night, took, during the time of it, a number of men with him, and as soon as it was dark, opened the trenches on the side towards the river. When this was done the water ran off in the night into the trenches, and the bed of the river through the city allowed men to walk along it." [1]

Anxiously the Jews within and the Persians without must have watched the gradual sinking of the water in the river-bed; still more anxiously must they have watched for any sign of suspicion or alarm within the doomed city. For "if the Babylonians had been aware of it beforehand," says Herodotus, "or had known what Cyrus was about, they would not have suffered the Persians to enter the city, but would have utterly destroyed them; for having shut all the little gates that lead down to the river, and mounting the walls that extend along the banks of the river, they would have caught them as in a net; whereas the Persians came upon them by surprise" (i. 191).

[1] Xenophon, *Cyro.* vii. 5, 15, 16.

Belshazzar and the lords who feasted with him were not, indeed (so we are told), without one solemn warning of their fate; for in the midst of their revelry, while they drank wine (out of the gold and silver cups which Nebuchadnezzar had taken from God's temple at Jerusalem)—in that same hour, while *they drank wine, and praised the gods of gold, and of silver, of brass, of iron, of wood, and of stone, . . . came forth fingers of a man's hand, and wrote over against the candlestick upon the plaister of the wall of the king's palace: and the king saw the part of the hand that wrote. Then the king's countenance was changed, and his thoughts troubled him. Astonied* (*i.e.* petrified) he *cried aloud to bring in the astrologers, the Chaldeans, and the soothsayers*, promising them great rewards if they could read the writing. But none could *read the writing, nor make known the interpretation thereof;* until at last the queen-mother, the Sultana Validé (perhaps the Nitocris of Herodotus), be-thought herself of that Daniel who had grown old in her father's service,—who had so wonderfully interpreted Nebuchadnezzar's dreams, and *dis-solved his doubts*, in days gone by. Coming into the banqueting-hall she addressed her son. " *O king, live for ever,"* she said. *"There is a man in thy kingdom, in whom is the spirit of the holy gods: and in the days of thy father, light and understanding, and wisdom, like the wisdom of the gods, was found in him: . . . now let Daniel be called, and he will shew the interpretation. Then was Daniel brought in before the king"* (Dan. v. 10-13).

Daniel must by this time have been an old man, but he seems to have lost none of his early directness and power. *" Let thy gifts be to thyself,"* he said, *" and give thy rewards to another ; yet I will read the writing unto the king, and make known to him the interpretation."* He reminded Belshazzar of the doom of Nebuchadnezzar. *" And thou his son, O Belshazzar, hast not humbled thine heart, though thou knewest all this."* And then he read the four Chaldean words, *"Mene, mene, tekel, upharsin,"* literally signifying "numbered, numbered, weighed, divided," which he interpreted to mean that God had *numbered* Belshazzar's kingdom and *finished* it, that he had been *weighed in the balance and found wanting,* that *his kingdom was divided and given to the Medes and Persians.*

The king, no doubt, did not believe in the

doom, or, believing, could not think it was so near. He loaded Daniel with gifts, and sent him away; but in that very night the awful message was fulfilled. *In that night was Belshazzar the king of the Chaldeans slain* (Dan. v. 30).

" The river,[1] my friends," Xenophon imagined Cyrus as saying to his assembled army, standing there in the darkness, " the river has yielded us a passage into the city; and let us boldly enter, fearing nothing within, but considering that these people, on whom we are now going to fall, are the same that we defeated when they had allies with them, and were all awake, sober, armed, and in order. We shall fall upon them at a time when many are asleep, many intoxicated, and all in confusion; and when they discover that we

---

[1] The river which, in the fourth year of King Zedekiah, had received the record of the city's coming destruction. " *The word which Jeremiah the prophet commanded Seraiah . . . when he went with Zedekiah the king of Judah into Babylon in the fourth year of his reign. And this Seraiah was a quiet prince* (in margin chief chamberlain). *So Jeremiah wrote in a book all the evil that should come upon Babylon,* commanding Seraiah to *bind a stone to it and cast it into the midst of Euphrates,* saying, " *Thus shall Babylon sink, and shall not rise.*"—Jer. li. 59.

are in the city, they will, by reason of their con-
sternation, be yet more unfit for service than they
now are. March, that we may surprise them
as little prepared as possible."

Of the hapless inhabitants of the devoted
city who were keeping holiday in her streets,
"some were struck down and killed, some fled, and
some raised a shout. . . . As a great clamour and
noise ensued, those who were within heard the
tumult, and as the king ordered them to see what
was the matter, some of them threw open the
gates and rushed out." . . . The invaders then
"burst in, and pursuing those who fled, and dealing blows amongst them, came up to the king,
and found him in a standing posture with his
sword drawn." [1]

Princes and soldiers, starting up, half drunk
and bewildered from their revel, had no time even
to attempt escape, before the Persian soldiery were
upon them. *The mighty men of Babylon*, in their
helplessness, *forbore to fight*. In vain now for
them to *set up the standard upon the walls of
Babylon, make the watch strong, set up the watch-
men, prepare the ambushes: for the Lord hath both*

[1] Xenophon, *Cyro.* vii. 5, 20-28.

devised and done that which he spake against the inhabitants of Babylon. "*O thou that dwellest upon many waters, abundant in treasures,*" cried Jeremiah, "*thine end is come, and the measure of thy covetousness*" (li. 12).

The huge city was *taken at one end* before the messengers could run to tell the other. Indeed, Herodotus assures us that "the inhabitants of the central parts (as the people who live in Babylon declare), long after the outer parts of the town were taken, knew nothing of what had chanced (for it happened to be a festival); but they continued dancing and revelling until they learned the capture but too certainly" (i. 191).

In their heat I will make their feasts, and I will make them drunken, that they may rejoice. . . . And I will make drunk the princes of Babylon, and her sages, her captains, and her rulers, and her mighty men: and they shall sleep a perpetual sleep (Jer. li. 39, 57).

So fell the mighty city Babylon. "Merodach, the great lord," says one of the British Museum cylinders of Cyrus, "beheld with joy the deeds of his vicegerent, who was righteous in hand and heart. . . . Without fighting or battle he caused

him to enter into Babylon."[1]   "*Come down, and
sit in the dust, O virgin daughter of Babylon; sit on
the ground: there is no throne, O daughter of the
Chaldeans,*" sang the exultant Jewish exiles ; "*for
thou shalt no more be called tender and delicate.
Take the millstones, and grind meal: uncover thy
locks, make bare the leg, uncover the thigh, pass over
the rivers. . . . Sit thou silent, and get thee into
darkness, O daughter of the Chaldeans: for thou
shalt no more be called The lady of kingdoms*" (Is.
xlvii. 1-5). With joy they welcomed Cyrus the
conqueror : "*Babylon is fallen, is fallen; and all
the graven images of her gods he hath broken unto
the ground,*" they cried (Is. xxi. 9).

At first, indeed, Cyrus did not himself take
command of the city. One of the generals of the
Median army which had helped him in his conquest (the "Darius" of Daniel VI.) *was made king
over the realm of the Chaldeans.* "Cyrus appointed
Gobryas to be governor in Babylon," says the
inscription. On his death, which happened in 536
B.C., Cyrus himself assumed the sovereignty ; and
one of his first acts was to issue a proclamation
that the Jews might go back to their native land.

[1] Smith, *Babylonia*, 158.

U

" *The Lord God of heaven hath given me all the kingdoms of the earth,*" Ezra makes him say; "*and he hath charged me to build him an house at Jerusalem, which is in Judah.   Who is there among you of all his people? his God be with him, and let him go up to Jerusalem*" (i. 2-3).   Then rose up the chief of the fathers of Judah and Benjamin . . . *to go up out of the captivity.*   They did not *go out with haste, nor go by flight* (Is. lii. 12), but *strengthened* with gold and silver, *with goods and with beasts and with precious things.*

Well might they cry " *Sing, O ye heavens; for the Lord hath done it : . . . That saith to the deep, Be dry; and I will dry up thy rivers : That saith of Cyrus, He is my shepherd, and shall perform all my pleasure; even saying to Jerusalem, Thou shalt be built; and to the temple, Thy foundation shall be laid*" (Is. xliv. 23-28).

" *When the Lord turned again the captivity of Zion, we were like them that dream,*" sang the Psalmist. " *Then was our mouth filled with laughter, and our tongue with singing : then said they among the heathen, The Lord hath done great things for them.   The Lord hath done great things for us, whereof we are glad. . . . They that sow in tears shall*

*reap in joy. He that goeth forth and weepeth,
bearing precious seed, shall doubtless come again with
rejoicing, bringing his sheaves with him* " (Ps. cxxvi.).

Here we may fitly end. The taking of Babylon
by Cyrus, the restoration of the Jewish exiles,
form "the very point," as Mr. Arnold has said,
"where Jewish history, caught in the current of
Cyrus's wars and policy, is carried into the great
open stream of the world's history, never again
to be separated from it." [1]

Cyrus died ten years after the taking of Babylon, in 529 B.C. He was succeeded by his son
Cambyses, the cruel conqueror of Egypt; and,
later, by Darius Hystaspes, who was perhaps,
next to Cyrus, the greatest king of Persia, but
who failed signally in his attempt to punish the
Greeks for helping their colonists in Asia Minor
to revolt against him. His was the army which
was defeated at Marathon (490 B.C.); and ten
years later his son Xerxes (the Ahasuerus of the
book of Esther) was also beaten back by the brave
Grecian troops.[2]   Of these things, and of the con-

---

[1] *Great Prophecy*, xiv.
[2] See Smith's *Dict. of Bible*, Art. *Ahasuerus*.

quest of Persia by Alexander the Great (332 B.C.), we read in Grecian history.

The Holy Land then passed from the *silver* monarchy of Persia to the *kingdom of brass* which, under Alexander, *bore rule over all the earth* (Dan. ii. 39). When that kingdom was broken up the Jews were ruled for one hundred years by the Ptolemies of Egypt, and after that, for half a century again by the Seleucidae, or kings of Syria, descendants of Alexander's general Seleucus. In 166 B.C. Judas Maccabæus delivered his countrymen from the Syrian tyrant Antiochus Epiphanes, and the Holy Land was for a century independent. But finally, in 63 B.C., Jerusalem was taken by the Roman general Pompey, and Judæa became part of that great empire, *strong as iron*, which *breaketh in pieces and subdueth all things* (Dan. ii. 40).[1]

Under the iron rule of Rome the Jews proved themselves restless and rebellious subjects; and

---

[1] These were the "four kingdoms" of Daniel's prophecy (ii.). "The common mode of treating Universal History," says Carlyle, "was to group the Aggregate Transactions of the Human Species into Four Monarchies: the Assyrian Monarchy of Nebuchadnezzar & Co.; the Persian of Cyrus & ditto; the Greek of Alexander; and lastly the Roman." The Fifth Mon-

at length, in 70 A.D., Jerusalem was again taken, after a long siege, by Titus ; the city was razed to the ground, the Temple was burnt, and the Jews were scattered abroad over all the earth—a people without a home, a nation without a country.

archy men of 1650 were so called because they proclaimed a "Fifth monarchy, by far the blessedest and the only real one,—the Monarchy of Jesus Christ, His Saints reigning for Him here on Earth,—if not He Himself."—*Cromwell*, iv. 27.

INDEX

THE END

Printed by R. & R. Clark, *Edinburgh.*

320